Becoming A Vessel
GOD CAN USE

Bethany House Books
by Donna Partow

Becoming a Vessel God Can Use
Families That Play Together Stay Together
How to Work With the One You Love (with Cameron Partow)
No More Lone Ranger Moms

9607

Becoming A Vessel
GOD CAN USE

Donna Partow

BETHANY HOUSE PUBLISHERS
MINNEAPOLIS, MINNESOTA 55438

Published by Bethany House Publishers
A Ministry of Bethany Fellowship, Inc.
11300 Hampshire Avenue South
Minneapolis, Minnesota 55438

Printed in the United States of America.

Library of Congress Cataloging-in-Publication Data

Partow, Donna.
    Becoming a vessel God can use / Donna Partow
        p.   cm.
    ISBN 1-55661-663-5
    1. Women—Religious life.   2. Spiritual life--Christianity.
I. Title.
BV4527.P37   1996
248.8'43—dc20   96-4431
                                                                CIP

To Lynne Rienstra, with love and admiration.
Thanks for modeling the life of a vessel God can use.
It has been beautiful to behold.

May God himself, the God of peace, sanctify you through and through. May your whole spirit, soul and body be kept blameless at the coming of our Lord Jesus Christ. The one who calls you is faithful and he will do it.

1 Thessalonians 5:23–24

DONNA PARTOW is a stay-at-home mom, a home-based business woman, and an enthusiastic home educator. She is the author of three previous books, *Homemade Business* (Focus on the Family, 1992), *No More Lone Ranger Moms* (Bethany House, 1995), and *How to Work With the One You Love* (Bethany House, 1995).

If your church sponsors an annual women's retreat, perhaps they would be interested in learning more about the author's special weekend program on "Becoming a Woman God Can Use." She is also available for luncheons and one-day events. For more information, contact:

Partow Communications
3764 N. Sawtooth Circle
Mesa, AZ 85215
(602) 807–3882

Or call toll-free

Interact Christian Speaker's Bureau
1–800–370–9932

Special Thanks

To my Heavenly Father, who graciously chooses to work through this imperfect vessel.

Bert Calland and the late Bill Calland, for unconditional love and uncompromising faith. Thanks for tilling the soil.

Bruce Bacon, who had the guts to tell me about Jesus and wouldn't take no for an answer.

Wendy Dawson, Chuck Garriott, Rob Rienstra, Eileen Riviello, and the rest of the youth leaders at Covenant Presbyterian Church. You had nerves of steel and faith to move mountains.

John and Shelley Julien and the members of New Life Presbyterian Church. Thanks for taking in a pair of vagabonds like Cameron and me. You gave and gave, knowing we had nothing to offer in return.

My sister, Nancy, who's been telling me for nearly thirty years: "It takes every kind of people." Sorry I didn't listen, Sis. Life would have been much easier if I had.

My lifeline: Debbie Stafford, Cathy Swope, Susie Sennewald, Nancy Martineau, Diane Lilly, and Charlene Cardona. Thanks for sharing the load.

My editorial committee: Beth Riley, Helen Sturm, Pauline Pace, and Bev Phillips. Thanks for putting in your two cents' worth; it was priceless.

The Thursday morning gang: Cindy Forsythe, Pauline Pace, Gail Rea, Aina Runzo, and Marcia Rupright. Thanks for "roughing it" with me.

My husband, as always, and my precious Leah. Thanks for behaving yourselves at Pinetop.

Steve Laube, who put the pen back in my hand. And the staff at Bethany House, who believed that pen could produce a message worth sharing.

Contents

Week One: Understanding

Understanding How and Why God Uses Imperfect Vessels

This Week's Focus Verse:

"For my thoughts are not your thoughts, neither are your ways my ways," declares the LORD. "As the heavens are higher than the earth, so are my ways higher than your ways and my thoughts than your thoughts."

Isaiah 55:8–9

Day One

Do I Have to Be Perfect?

If you're looking for a book by one of today's most admired Christian women, an ideal Christian wife who hasn't argued with her husband in over twenty years . . .

If you want know-how from an adoring mother who never raises her voice, has perfectly disciplined children, and maintains a spotlessly clean house—I mean a woman whose domestic skills put Martha Stewart to shame . . .

If you want to read words of wisdom from a woman with color-coded closets, who not only makes her own clothes but gives fabulous handmade gifts for every occasion; a woman who rises at the crack of dawn, jogs five miles, and returns home in time to bake bread from scratch—all before her husband leaves for work . . .

If you want to get the inside track from a woman who is universally adored and admired by everyone who meets her . . .

If you want to follow in the footsteps of a woman who has conducted neighborhood Bible studies for twenty-five years and led 400 women to Christ . . .

Quick, do not delay! Put this book down immediately! You must have me confused with some other Christian author!

If, on the other hand, you're willing to read a book written by a woman who has been known to blow it *big time*, a woman who, by *Total Woman* standards, would have to be labeled 2%. If you're willing to spend some time with a woman known to leave her dishes unwashed for several days, and who, even as she writes these words, is watching her five-year-old daughter clean the windows with furniture polish, then pour yourself a cup of coffee and take a seat. We're about to begin an exciting journey together.

This book is not about becoming like *me*. It's not about how I've got it all figured out and now I can impart to you the "Ten Surefire Steps to Super-Spirituality." I did not write this book because I consider myself a shining example of a vessel God can use—far from it. I wrote this book because becoming a vessel God can use has been a far more difficult and personally painful journey than I ever imagined possible, and I want to minister out of that pain. I want to comfort you with the comfort I have received.

The exciting truth I want you to grab hold of is this: God can use imperfect vessels like you and me. In fact, he often delights in choosing the most unlikely people to accomplish his purposes in this world. Everyone around you may consider you the least likely job candidate, but fortunately, God works as his own employment recruiter! No matter who you are, if you will yield your life to God, you can become a vessel God can use.

I urge you to set aside time *daily* during the next ten weeks to concentrate on your relationship with your heavenly Father. The study should only require 20–30 minutes per day, five days a week. Then, once a week, you should join with a small group of women to review the discussion questions, to pray and encourage one another, and to hold one another accountable. Be sure to place top-priority on memorizing your weekly verse. To make it easier, you'll find cutout verse cards at the back of the book. Carry these cards in your purse and review them when you are on the run. You can also make an extra set to post in a conspicuous place—like the refrigerator door or over the sink where you do dishes or wash your face each morning.

I hope you will make this study a genuine priority in your life. The housecleaning will wait; someone else can bake the brownies for a while; all your favorite TV shows will still be there at the end of the journey. Nevertheless, I understand that hectic weeks may come and you'll find it difficult to complete each day's study. In those instances, let me suggest that you focus on Day 1, because it introduces the theme, and Day 5, because it crystalizes the week's study. Then, as time permits, complete the remaining days for a fuller understanding of the material. Again, the ideal approach is to complete each day's study on a daily basis, rather than cramming on the morning of your weekly small group.

Working through this book won't make you perfect and it won't be easy, but I promise you will gain a fuller understanding of the price and the possibilities, the challenges and the joys of *Becoming a Vessel God Can Use.*

1. Do you have to be perfect to become a vessel God can use? How important are other people's opinions of your qualifications?

2. In what ways has God already used you to make a difference in other people's lives? List those who come to mind by name and thank God for the privilege of being a vessel used by him.

3. Write out a prayer of commitment to the Lord, stating your intentions of working through this material to gain a fuller understanding of what it means to be a vessel he can use.

4. Cut out the memory verse cards and get started!

5. If you are not working through this book as part of a small group, find a friend who will work through it with you. Plan a time to get together each week for prayer, encouragement, and accountability.

6. What key lesson did you glean from today's study?

To recap:

- You do not have to be perfect to become a vessel God can use.
- The amount of spiritual growth you enjoy as a result of this study will be a direct result of the amount of time, prayer, and effort you invest.

Day Two

Is There a Place for Me?

D o you ever wonder where you fit in to God's grand plan? Do you ever wonder if there really is a place for you? Maybe when you think about the kind of vessel you are, words like "chipped, cracked, broken, and dirty" come to mind. Maybe you feel like a dusty old jar forgotten on the shelf or an ugly water jug abandoned by the side of the road. Maybe you see yourself as a crystal vase— you look good from a distance and people admire you, but a closer look reveals cracks from top to bottom. You couldn't hold water if you tried, let alone provide life to another living being.

Maybe you picked up this book on becoming a vessel God can use and thought *I don't even know what kind of vessel I am—how can God use me when I don't even know what I'm useful for?* If so, you are not alone. When I taught this ten-week study for the first time, I quickly discovered that many women weren't sure what kind of vessel they were; not sure how or where God could use them. Some of the women were looking for a course on spiritual gifts, and while there are certainly some excellent (and very valuable) books on discovering your gifts and talents—this isn't one of them. Do you know why? Because if you are not living your life as a vessel God can use, understanding your gifts won't *address the real problem.* Your turning point will come when you understand how and why God works through frail human vessels like us. Once you understand those two things, God will use you in astounding ways—ways that a hundred spiritual gift courses could never prepare you for. When you come to grips with the truth that God's thoughts are not like your thoughts and your ways are not his ways, I promise you will be transformed into a vessel he can use. (*Then* you can take a spiritual gifts class and get much more from it. Check out the book *Discovering Your Spiritual Gifts* by Don and Katie Fortune, published by Chosen Books.)

When I became a Christian, I had very clear ideas about what my gifts were and how I could be useful to God. My attitude was: God has done so much for me, I want to do things for him in return. Now everybody stand back and watch me work. Unfortunately, my focus was on me and the great things *I* was going to accomplish for God, rather than on God and the great things he wanted to accomplish *through* me. Understanding the difference between those two approaches to ministry is at the heart of this study.

For years, I wondered, "Why does God use everyone else? What's wrong with me?" Deep in my heart of hearts, I longed for the significance that can only come when our lives are a channel through which God can work. I wondered why some women were used in such powerful ways to minister to others, while I felt so ineffective.

Mind you, it's not that I didn't try. Far from it. One thing I do have is an abundance of energy and a willing spirit. I poured myself into every ministry opportunity that came along. I taught Vacation Bible School to three- and four-year-olds. I baked casseroles and cookies as part of the Fellowship Committee. I even tried my hand at Jell-O molds—not a pretty sight. I invited newcomers to my home on behalf of the Hospitality Committee. I planned wild and crazy church socials as part of the Social Committee. (Well, crazy by *our* church's standards!)

My Sunday school teaching experience ranged from kindergartners to junior high and high school students. Then I became a volunteer youth leader and went well beyond Sunday mornings. I invited the students and their parents to my home. I met with them one-on-one throughout the week. I developed customized Bible studies tailored to their current crises. I visited them on the job. (It was easy to find them; all teenagers work at the mall, you know.) I peddled influence to *get* them jobs. I even hired them to work around my house. I took them to Christian rock concerts and went camping in the rain. (I urge you to avoid that last experience at all costs.)

I volunteered to head up the Missions Committee. I read dozens of books on the how's and the why's, the history and the future of missions. My husband and I attended missionary dinners; we had missionaries in our home, and we sent monthly support to missionaries. (Still do!) I faithfully corresponded with a dozen missionary families and even managed to convince some teenagers to go on short-term mission trips.

My husband and I hosted weekly small group Bible studies in our home for nearly a decade. We worked for the Billy Graham Crusade when it came to town and tried to be mini-evangelists. I memorized the plan of salvation and all the right scriptures a la *Evangelism Explosion*. I dropped hints to the neighbors and co-workers every day of the week. I debated the merits of Christianity with an apologetic flair that would have put Josh McDowell to shame. I enthusiastically touted the joys of the Christian life. (Didn't live 'em, just touted 'em.) I invited scores of people to church, to the Crusade, anywhere I thought God might "do his thing."

Another pet project was my family. I've got a mom, a dad, seven older brothers and sisters, who brought with them a parade of spouses, lovers, nieces, nephews, in-laws—you name it. I spent countless hours in agonized prayer over them. I planned and plotted; I manipulated people and events. On several occasions, I did a most remarkable imitation of the Holy Spirit as I witnessed to them and nearly dragged them into the Kingdom. Finally, God showed forth his mercy upon my family—he moved me out-of-state.

Well, that's not even the half of it. As you can see, I certainly wasn't lacking in zeal. (Tact has always been in short supply, though.) Yet, no matter how hard I tried, it rarely seemed God was really using me in people's lives. Oh, there were odd breakthroughs here and there. Occasionally, it looked like something I'd said or done had made a difference. But in proportion to the amount of effort I was pouring forth, the returns were dismal.

In fact, God usually worked in spite of me, not because of me. I felt frustrated and exhausted. I had scattered my energies in a thousand different directions, but saw little fruit. The only tangible results were the bitterness that enveloped me and the wake of confused, frustrated, and often angry people I left behind.

So I stopped.

I stopped the committees and the Bible studies, the Sunday school and the mission society. I stopped baking casseroles and sending note cards. I stopped the whirlwind. Funny thing, though, no one seemed to mind. So I stopped going to church altogether. Actually, I stopped living, period. Sure, I inhaled and exhaled, even mustered up a pulse. But, in truth, I had withdrawn from life: I had effectively cut myself off from everyone and everything. *I thought it would hurt less. I was wrong.* The hours that were once filled with activity, however fruitless, were now filled with depression and despair.

Clearly, this new approach wasn't working, either. So I came up with a novel ideal. I decided to study my Bible. I was determined to uncover what the heroes of the Bible had in common. What was it that made them *so great* that the God of the universe hired them to "get the job done" down here on earth?

Do you know what I discovered? I discovered a collection of the most *unlikely people* imaginable. From homemakers and prophets to prostitutes and murderers, God was able to work through anyone who firmly believed he could and would use imperfect vessels. As I have gradually released my own agenda and turned myself—broken, imperfect vessel that I am—over to God, he has begun to work through my life. This book you hold in your hands is one of the fruits of that process.

Do you want to be a vessel God can use? Let go of your plans to do great things for God and cling to the truth that God is able to work through an imperfect vessel like you. This study will guide you through that process. It begins with an understanding of who God really is and who you are as his creation. It's a process that involves accepting the purpose for which God created you, even if it's not the life you envisioned for yourself. It requires being emptied of yourself and allowing God to cleanse you and fill you anew. Then, and only then, will you have anything to give in ministry to others. As you learn to become a moldable, usable vessel in the hands of God, you'll discover that ministry is no longer a burden, no longer a list of things *you have to do*. Rather, it's a simple matter of listening for God's voice, then following where he leads.

At the end of this book you will find a summary of the "Five Requirements for Becoming a Vessel God Can Use." I encourage you to turn there often to review them throughout the course of this study. Allow these principles to seep down into your soul and actually become part of your being, *your vessel*. In this way, the heart of the study will remain with you for years to come—and isn't that what you want to happen when you undertake a study like this? Whenever you find yourself out of step with God, you can stop and mentally go through the "Five Requirements" to discover where you have gotten off track.

1. Imagine yourself as a vessel. Describe what you see.

2. Which is more important: understanding your spiritual gifts or understanding the one who imparts spiritual gifts? Why?

3. What is the difference between accomplishing things for God and allowing him to accomplish his work through you?

4. Which of the above approaches best describes your Christian life so far?

5. What key lesson did you glean from today's study?

To recap:

- Understanding what God wants to accomplish through your life is far more important than deciding what you think you can accomplish for him.
- The key to effective ministry is understanding how and why God works through imperfect vessels like us.

Day Three

Gideon, You're the One!

H ere is an amazing biblical account of how God chooses unlikely vessels to accomplish his purposes:

The angel of the LORD came and sat down under the oak in
Ophrah that belonged to Joash the Abiezrite, where his son Gideon was threshing wheat in a winepress to keep it from the Midianites. When the angel of the LORD appeared to Gideon, he
said, "The LORD is with you, mighty warrior."

"But sir," Gideon replied, "if the LORD is with us, why has
all this happened to us? Where are all his wonders that our fathers told us about when they said, 'Did not the LORD bring us
up out of Egypt?' But now the LORD has abandoned us and put
us into the hand of Midian."

The LORD turned to him and said, "Go in the strength you
have and save Israel out of Midian's hand. Am I not sending
you?"

"But Lord," Gideon asked, "how can I save Israel? My clan
is the weakest in Manasseh, and I am the least in my family."

The LORD answered, "I will be with you, and you will strike
down all the Midianites as if they were but one man."

Judges 6:11–16

Gideon's recruitment carries some important lessons:

- *God is not looking for self-confident people.* Gideon was just a
farmer, trying to put food on the table. He considered himself
the least of a weak bunch. And he wasn't exactly bubbling over
with a winning attitude, either. Notice how he blames God for
getting the Israelites into their current predicament and has major doubts about God's willingness or desire to save them. Nevertheless, Gideon was God's man for the job.

22

- *God isn't interested in our excuses.* There's no need for us to waste God's time pointing out our weaknesses or the obstacles we face. He knows our circumstances far better than we do ourselves. God knows you fully; he knows what you are capable of doing through the power of the Holy Spirit. He will only call you to complete a job he knows you can handle *with His power.* When God calls us to obey, all he wants is our obedience and he'll handle the details.

- *Don't expect all the answers up front.* Gideon had no idea whether or not his father would come to his defense. It was entirely possible that his father might have *led the charge* to execute him; after all, this was an overwhelming show of defiance. In essence, Gideon said, "In your face, Dad. I reject your religion, your position, and everything you stand for." Only God knew the outcome; Gideon didn't. We are responsible for our choices; God is responsible for the results.

The Lord told Gideon, "Go in the strength you have. . . . Am I not sending you?" We must do the same, even if we don't think our strength is sufficient. The Coast Guard has a motto we would do well to adopt. It says, "You must go out; you don't have to come back." So go out—step out in obedience to God—and let God worry about whether or not you come back.

Isn't it amazing how, once we get on board with what God is doing, we expect everyone else to fall in line? We see this truth played out vividly in the way the Israelite leaders react when Gideon obeyed God:

> They asked each other, "Who did this?"
>
> When they carefully investigated, they were told, "Gideon son of Joash did it."
>
> The men of the town demanded of Joash, "Bring out your son. He must die, because he has broken down Baal's altar and cut down the Asherah pole beside it."
>
> But Joash replied to the hostile crowd around him, "Are you going to plead Baal's cause? Are you trying to save him? Whoever fights for him shall be put to death by morning! If Baal really is a god, he can defend himself when someone breaks down his altar."
> Judges 6:29–31

- *Don't Listen for the Cheering Section.* The truth is, if you expect people to cheer you on, you will end up disappointed. Don't count on getting support when you step out in obedience to Christ—not even from your own family or so-called religious leaders. It is entirely possible that you'll face fierce opposition as you allow God to accomplish his purposes through you. Did Gideon receive *praise* for his giant leap of faith? Far from it! All he heard was criticism and *death threats*. God knows exactly what he can achieve through you, if you are willing to do as he directs. Will you take up the challenge? Great—but don't listen for the cheering section.

1. What specific objections did Gideon raise when God called on him to perform a tough assignment? Were they legitimate?

2. What four lessons do we learn from the recruitment of Gideon?

3. What are some limitations you point out to God when he asks you to follow him in obedience?

4. Can you recall an occasion when you obeyed God and received nothing but criticism from the people around you? Describe.

5. What key lesson did you glean from today's study?

To recap:

- God fully knows you and the circumstances you face.
- God will only call you to complete a job he knows you can handle by his power.
- You must go "in the strength you have"—even if you don't think it's enough.
- Don't expect people to support you when you step out in obedience to God.
- Remember who sends you.

Day Four

The Least Likely Job Candidate

S everal years ago, God placed the following help-wanted ad in a nationwide newspaper:

> CHUTZBA. Powerful employer looking for person with lots of chutzba to share the gospel with beautiful, young Jewish girl. All applicants welcome: any age, gender, or race may qualify. Must be willing to offend Jewish sensibilities. Contact God via prayer if interested in a tough assignment.

Okay, so God didn't really take out a help-wanted ad, but if he did, that's how it would have read. You see, at the time, a young Jewish girl named Suzanne was in desperate circumstances. Suzanne tells her story:

"My fiancé had gotten a baseball scholarship to a leading university, so I decided to study there, too. The first year was a blur of ditching class, toga parties, and wild and crazy dorm life. Not much school education, but life education of a sort. I had always been a spiritual person. I had gone to Hebrew school and I prayed a lot. But there was no spiritual *life*.

"I can remember in high school, looking at books on witchcraft in the school library. I even took a course on Eastern religion and learned transcendental meditation. Then I met an intriguing man who told me the most incredible stories of his life-after-death and other amazing spiritual experiences. It was all very compelling. Then he gave me a book called *Rebirthing in the New Age* and started inviting me to meetings at million-dollar homes overlooking the ocean. They had these hot-tub parties, where you'd go through hypnosis and be re-born in the hot tub. He later told me they did LSD, too.

"All the while, I was surrounded by really neat Christians, like the assistant baseball coach, and another ball player and his father.

They really demonstrated love to me. I later found out they were praying for me all along. But no one ever told me about Jesus or confronted me with his claims to be the Jewish Messiah. I guess they didn't want to offend me.

"I was on the verge of attending the New Age group, when I got to the last chapter of the *Rebirthing* book. It talked about Jesus, but only as a great prophet and enlightened teacher. It didn't matter. Something about this Jesus just leaped out at me from the page. It was incredible, because as a Jew, Jesus was someone I just never thought about."

Around this time, Suzanne broke up with her boyfriend—the man everyone had expected her to marry for as long as she could remember. The decision was painful to make; the news even harder to hear. Her boyfriend began stalking her. She locked herself in her dorm room and was afraid to even answer the phone. Guilt and confusion overcame her, as she wandered to the very brink of a nervous breakdown. "I didn't eat or sleep for nearly a week. I just cried day and night. Finally, I decided to get a Bible. I'd never seen one and had no idea where to get one. I went to a regular bookstore. Sure enough, there it was. Then I found the Trinity Broadcasting Network and I kept Christian TV going twenty-four hours a day.

"I couldn't believe what I was discovering. The first half of the Bible was filled with truths I already believed. Here were the patriarchs and the prophets, old familiar voices. Then I started reading about the promised Messiah. When I stumbled onto Isaiah 53, I just couldn't believe it. I knew Jesus was the one we'd been waiting for. But, wait, what would my family say? How could I hurt them like this?

"I cried out to God and pleaded with him to speak to me. I prayed, 'God, I don't want to turn my back on the faith you've given me. I don't want to be misled. Please, please help me.' It was two o'clock in the morning. I was sitting in the middle of the floor in my bathrobe, wrapped in a comforter. The only light came from the flickering TV screen. There was a woman singing on TV. She suddenly pointed to the camera and said, 'There's a young girl out there. You're sitting in the pitch black and it's the middle of the night. I know it's day here, but our show is taped. It's night where you are. You're sitting in your living room in your bathrobe, wrapped in a comforter. You are calling out to God and he has heard your prayers, sweetheart. He will never leave you. It's gonna be all right. God has heard you.' "

The woman on the screen was Tammy Faye Baker.

At that moment, Suzanne accepted Christ. "I felt like somebody was pouring buckets of cool refreshing water over my entire body, from my head down to my feet, and it just kept coming. It snapped me out of the despair and depression. I could feel the cleansing. I knew. I just knew."

She recalls, "Later I heard nothing but criticism of Tammy Baker and the PTL Club. She seemed to be the laughingstock of Christianity. This happened right in the middle of the scandal, too. For some reason, though, her makeup and hair didn't bother me. All the makeup in the world couldn't stand in the way of what God was doing in my life. I'd come to the breaking point. I was either gonna grab the lifeline or fall off the edge."

Here's the point: God can use anyone he wants! He's God. Suzanne was surrounded by sincere, loving Christians who genuinely cared about her. Highly respected campus ministries were in full-swing all around her. But God didn't use them for this assignment. That's not to say they didn't have an effective ministry in many other areas. However, in this particular case, he was looking for someone whose sole qualification was chutzba. And he found it in one Tammy Faye Baker.

Now, if I were God's employment recruiter, and this woman strutted her stuff in the door, the words "wrong, wrong, wrong" would immediately spring to mind. Yet, God used her. I'm not endorsing or condemning Tammy Faye Baker. I'm just pointing out that she appears to be a most *unlikely vessel*. And that's precisely the *power* in this story. There's no human explanation possible—the perfect scenario for giving God 100% of the glory. And that's the way he requires it.

It also reminds us that even when we stumble and fall, God can still use us, because our lives become a warning to others that we are all vulnerable to Satan's attack. When we turn our hearts back to him, we can know with confidence that God will restore us. As our memory verse for this week reminds us: "The eyes of the Lord range throughout the earth to strengthen those whose hearts are fully committed to him."

1. Does it surprise you that God chose to use a controversial figure, a woman embroiled in public scandal, to bring a hurting soul into the Kingdom? Why or why not?

2. Is there anything you can ever do that will render you "unusable" to God?

3. Who are some unlikely people God has used to accomplish his work in your life? Recall the circumstances and how they changed you.

4. What key lesson did you glean today?

5. What was "This Week's Focus"?

To recap:

- When God wants to accomplish a task on earth through human vessels, he can choose anyone he pleases.
- God often chooses the most unlikely job candidate, so that he alone receives the glory.

Day Five

Will the Imperfect Please Step Forward?

During this week you have encountered both biblical and contemporary examples of vessels God used. The basic premise of this entire book—a premise solidly based on the evidence of Scripture—is that God works through imperfect vessels who acknowledge their total dependence on him, even if they are people the world would never choose. We'll be exploring that theme throughout the book, but just to get you started, read through the following list of unlikely people God used to accomplish his purposes:

- Jacob, a deceiver and runaway who had to work fourteen years to get the wife he wanted, to father the nation of Israel.
- Joseph, a bragging, spoiled-rotten brat turned slave and ex-convict, to save his family (the twelve tribes of Israel and the ancestors of Christ).
- Moses, a murderer turned shepherd—a man so timid he told God to look elsewhere—to lead Israel out of bondage and to the edge of the promised land.
- Jephthah, son of a prostitute, to deliver Israel from the Ammonites.
- Rahab, a prostitute, a woman who lived a morally bankrupt life in a morally bankrupt culture—to play a pivotal role in helping the Israelites take the promised land.
- Hannah, a barren housewife, to be the mother of Samuel—one of the greatest prophets of the Old Testament.
- Eli, a man who blew it *big-time* with his own children (Hophni and Phinehas) to be the spiritual father of Samuel, who became the spiritual father/mentor of David.
- David, a humble shepherd boy and youngest in his family, who later committed adultery and murder, to be Israel's greatest king

and to pen many of the most beautiful, comforting, and inspiring passages of Scripture.

- Esther, a slave girl married to a Gentile, to save God's people from an impending massacre. (Remember, women were not held in high esteem in those days—and marriage to Gentiles was strongly condemned.)
- Mary, an unmarried peasant girl, to be the mother of Jesus.
- Matthew, a despised tax collector and symbol of Israel's oppressors, to be an apostle and writer of the first book of the New Testament.
- Peter, a hot-tempered working-class guy, a fisherman, to be an apostle, leader of the early Church, and writer of two New Testament letters.
- Paul, vicious persecutor of the early Church and approving witness of the stoning of the first Christian martyr, to take the Gospel to the Gentiles and write more New Testament books than any other author.

We have already seen *how* God uses imperfect vessels. The question remains: why? Why doesn't God choose Mr. and Mrs. Perfect? First, because the Bible says *all have sinned and fall short of the glory of God.* Those people who claim to be perfect—who claim to be without sin—are deceiving themselves and the truth is not in them.

Second, in choosing these unlikely vessels—something the world would consider foolish—God shows that even his seemingly foolish ideas are wiser than man's wisdom. When people behold something *only God can do*—like getting the job done through imperfect people—their eyes turn heavenward. God receives glory and man is restored to a right relationship with his Creator.

Let's consider how some of the scenarios above could have played out differently—how people could have seized the glory for themselves. Jacob could have been such a delight to Isaac that his father would have willingly given him a blessing. He never would have fled; he never would have endured hard labor under Laban. He would have married the girl next door and had children in the usual way. What a lucky guy! Ho-hum.

Moses could have remained in Pharaoh's house and peddled his influence to sneak weapons to the Hebrew slaves. He could have secretly trained an army of guerrilla fighters to rise up in bloody rebellion against their Egyptian masters. Thousands would have died; some would have naturally escaped. No plagues, no parting of the Red Sea, just another traitor in Pharaoh's court. Ho-hum.

Eli could have been the perfect father, chosen to train Samuel because he had done such a superior job with his own sons. God wouldn't have had to chat with Samuel in the night; Eli would have taught him everything he needed to know about God's will and God's ways. Not much excitement there!

Jesus could have chosen twelve of the most brilliant, powerful, and well-respected Pharisees to be his disciples. With their incredible knowledge of the Old Testament, coupled with the power they held over the people, they could have convinced the Jewish people Jesus was their Messiah. Remember, it was the Pharisees who convinced the crowd to cry, "crucify him," so they had plenty of influence. Why bother with uneducated fishermen and lowly tax collectors? For that matter, why bother with the Cross?

Well, you get the idea. The answer to all these hypothetical why's is *because God alone deserves all the glory*. As you begin to understand how and why God uses imperfect vessels, you will gain increased confidence to walk by faith, knowing God can and *will* use you.

1. Look up one of the "unlikely vessels" listed in today's study. Summarize their story below, noting what made them appear unlikely—and how that resulted in God receiving special glory.

2. Look back on your life. Recall the people God has used as vessels to minister to you. Were any of them perfect? List their names and how they were used. Try to recall at least five.

3. Wouldn't you love to receive a letter from a long-lost someone, recounting how God used you to make a difference in his or her life? Of course you would! Well, take the time right now to bring that kind of joy into someone's life. See how many of the people listed above you can track down—it may be impossible in some cases. Write an encouraging note to at least one.

4. What key lesson did you glean from today's study?

5. What was "This Week's Focus"?

To recap:

- Throughout history God chose imperfect vessels to accomplish his purposes.
- God can work through your life even though you are an imperfect vessel.

Week Two: Depending

Learning to Depend On God Alone and Walk In "God-Confidence"

This Week's Focus Verse:

For the eyes of the LORD range throughout the earth to strengthen those whose hearts are fully committed to him.

2 Chronicles 16:9

Day One

God-Confidence

What are some ways that you evaluate the likely outcome of a set of circumstances? One way is to look within yourself to see what your internal resources are. The answer you come up with is largely dependent upon your self-image, that is, how you view yourself and your abilities. The life of Gideon clearly demonstrated that a positive self-image is definitely *not* a prerequisite for serving God. In fact, self-confidence is often a major hindrance to becoming a vessel God can use. That's because *self-confidence* is the result of trusting in your own ability to handle people and circumstances.

By contrast, *God-confidence* is trust in God's ability to work through you to shape people and circumstances. When you have God-confidence, you can forget about your own strengths and weaknesses, knowing that God can get the job done, regardless. When you have God-confidence, you are freed from both pride and self-recrimination. You can focus on the job at hand and on the needs of others, leaving the results with God, where they belong.

Do you understand the difference between those two concepts? It's simple: one focuses on self, the other focuses on God. One focuses on temporal results; the other focuses on eternal rewards. Far better to accomplish one thing—touch *one life*—for eternity, by walking in God-confidence, than to accomplish great things by the world's standards, only to earn the applause of men. It will be a fearful moment for men who've built huge churches *on personal charisma* when they stand before the throne and God says their impressive numbers were just so much hay and stubble. What a joyous moment for the humble housewife who quietly ministered to the women of her neighborhood, because she did it for God's glory and by his power. Her reward will be great.

Which matters more to you? Temporary *results* or eternal *rewards*?

In 2 Chronicles 16:8–9, we discover a vivid contrast between self-confidence and God-confidence. When King Asa relied on the Lord to bring about victory, he was able to defeat the mighty armies of the Cushites and the Libyans, because he acted in God-confidence. In his most recent battle with Judah's enemies, however, he relied on his own cleverness and even turned to pagan nations for help. He acted out of self-confidence and here's how the Bible sums it up:

> Were not the Cushites and Libyans a mighty army with great numbers of chariots and horsemen? Yet when you relied on the LORD, he delivered them into your hand. For the eyes of the LORD range throughout the earth to strengthen those whose hearts are fully committed to him. You have done a foolish thing, and from now on you will be at war.   2 Chronicles 16:8–9

The *NIV Life Application Bible* (Zondervan Publishing House) adds this footnote:

> Judah and Israel never learned. Although God had delivered them even when they were outnumbered (13:3 ff; 14:9 ff), they repeatedly sought help from pagan nations rather than God. That Asa sought help from Aram was evidence of national spiritual decline. With help from God alone, Asa had defeated the Cushites in open battle. But his confidence in God had slipped, and now he sought only a human solution to his problem. It is not a sin to use human means to solve our problems. It is a sin to trust them more than we trust God, to think they are better than God's ways, or to leave God completely out of the picture.

The same is true for us today. When we rely on ourselves or look for merely human solutions—forgetting about the God factor—we are acting foolishly. As a result of our prideful attitude, we end up at war with the people around us. Why are we so foolish to look to ourselves and our own resources, when God *delights* in putting his resources to work on our behalf? When we place our confidence in God and God alone, he promises to strengthen us and do battle on our behalf (Exodus 14:14). That's the best battle plan of all.

1. The Lord said that King Asa (and the people) had done a foolish

thing. What was it?

2. What was the outcome of their foolish decision?

3. What's your understanding of the difference between self-confidence and God-confidence?

4. Which adjective best describes you: self-confident or God-confident? Give specific reasons for your answer.

5. What key lesson did you glean from today's study?

To recap:

- Self-confidence is trust in my own ability to handle people and circumstances.
- God-confidence is trust in God's ability to work through me to shape people and circumstances. When I have God-confidence, I can forget about myself and focus on the job at hand.

Day Two

What's So Special About Rahab?

F or the next few days, we're going to take a long, hard look at the life of Rahab. She happens to be one of my favorite people in the Bible, so I hope you will find this consideration of her life an inspiring experience. For today, your assignment is simply to read and re-read the passage below. Then, note everything you learn about Rahab: her career, her character, her courage, and her faith. Here's how she bursts onto the Bible scene:

> Then Joshua son of Nun secretly sent two spies from Shittim. "Go, look over the land," he said, "especially Jericho." So they went and entered the house of a prostitute named Rahab and stayed there.
>
> The king of Jericho was told, "Look! Some of the Israelites have come here tonight to spy out the land." So the king of Jericho sent this message to Rahab, "Bring out the men who came to you and entered your house, because they have come to spy out the whole land."
>
> But the woman had taken the two men and hidden them. She said, "Yes, the men came to me, but I did not know where they had come from. At dusk, when it was time to close the city gate, the men left. I don't know which way they went. Go after them quickly. You may catch up with them." (But she had taken them up to the roof and hidden them under the stalks of flax she had laid out on the roof.) So the men set out in pursuit of the spies on the road that leads to the fords of the Jordan, and as soon as the pursuers had gone out, the gate was shut.
>
> Before the spies lay down for the night, she went up on the roof and said to them, "I know that the LORD has given this land to you and that a great fear of you has fallen on us, so that all who live in this country are melting in fear because of you. We

have heard how the Lᴏʀᴅ dried up the water of the Red Sea for you when you came out of Egypt, and what you did to Sihon and Og, the two kings of the Amorites east of the Jordan, whom you completely destroyed. When we heard of it, our hearts sank and everyone's courage failed because of you, for the Lᴏʀᴅ your God is God in heaven above and on the earth below.

"Now then, please swear to me by the Lᴏʀᴅ that you will show kindness to my family, because I have shown kindness to you. Give me a sure sign that you will spare the lives of my father and mother, my brothers and sisters, and all who belong to them, and that you will save us from death."

"Our lives for your lives!" the men assured her. "If you don't tell what we are doing, we will treat you kindly and faithfully when the Lᴏʀᴅ gives us the land."

So she let them down by a rope through the window, for the house she lived in was part of the city wall. Now she had said to them, "Go to the hills so the pursuers will not find you. Hide yourselves there three days until they return, and then go on your way."

The men said to her, "This oath you made us swear will not be binding on us unless, when we enter the land, you have tied this scarlet cord in the window through which you let us down, and unless you have brought your father and mother, your brothers and all your family into your house. If anyone goes outside your house into the street, his blood will be on his own head; we will not be responsible. As for anyone who is in the house with you, his blood will be on our head if a hand is laid on him. But if you tell what we are doing, we will be released from the oath you made us swear."

"Agreed," she replied. "Let it be as you say." So she sent them away and they departed. And she tied the scarlet cord in the window.

When they left, they went into the hills and stayed there three days, until the pursuers had searched all along the road and returned without finding them.   Joshua 2:1–22

1. What observations can you make about Rahab, based on your reading of the passage? (There are no right or wrong answers; just react to the Bible text.) Consider her career, her character, her

courage, and her faith.

2. What key lesson did you glean from today's study?

To recap:

- A person's career does not tell the whole story about who they are.
- The most unlikely people can demonstrate character, courage, and faith.

Day Three

Rahab Had Total God-Confidence

The Bible doesn't tell us much about who Rahab was, other than the fact that she was a prostitute. We do, however, learn quite a bit about what she believed—and what she did about that belief. Her words reveal her heart: "For I know that the Lord has given this land to you . . . The Lord your God is God in heaven above and on the earth below."

Now, that's an incredible statement coming from the mouth of Rahab. She lived a morally bankrupt life in a morally bankrupt, pagan culture. She had never witnessed even one of God's miracles. She had never received even one of his promises or blessings. Yet, she wholeheartedly believed that he could perform miracles. She wholeheartedly believed that his promises concerning the Israelites would come to pass. That's a lot more than most Israelites believed.

Rahab is a model of faith for us, for at least four reasons:

- *She took God at his Word.* When God said the Israelites were to inhabit the land, Rahab considered it as good as done. In short she had total God-confidence. What else could explain her actions? Why else would she be willing to risk her life to serve this God whom she really knew very little about? Where could she have found the courage to defy her own king and protect the spies from the authorities? Do you think she received direct orders from the King of Jericho every day of the week? This was a pivotal moment in her life, requiring a huge leap of faith. She knew she was committing treason. She knew the penalty for treason was certain death. There's only one explanation: she took God at his Word.

Do you have that much faith? If the President of the United States *commanded you* to do something, would you defy him? If the

President of the United States sent a contingent of marines to your front door, asking you to send out two men you were hiding, what would you do? I suspect the vast majority of Christians *would send them out*. We have only to look at Germany in the 1930s as an example. Very few Christians were willing to defy Hitler. Perhaps you can think of a few examples closer to home.

- *She went against the crowd.* While all the other residents of Jericho prepared to do battle with the Israelites, Rahab prepared to protect them. She believed God would do what he said he would do, so she was willing to turn her back on the life she'd led and the people she had lived among. How about us? Do we have enough faith to go against the crowd? In my case, God has called me to go against the crowd by home-schooling my daughter. Even though many people in my neighborhood—and even in my church—are critical of my decision, I know I must obey God rather than men.

How about you? Can you think of *even one area* in your life where you are going against the crowd? If not, perhaps you are being conformed to this world, rather than being transformed by the renewing of your mind (Romans 12:2).

- *Rahab believed God and she* did *something about it.* Rahab's faith translated into tangible action: she hid the spies and *then helped them escape.* She took action, even to the point of laying her life on the line. Rahab believed God, that's why she was willing to do whatever she could to further God's agenda. That's why she was willing to be *a vessel God could use.*

How does your faith translate into tangible action? Again, can you think of one specific action you've taken in response to believing God?

- *Rahab believed God would take care of her.* How else could she have entrusted her very life into the hands of her enemies? Yes, the Israelites were her enemies. I don't think she trusted these men she had just met; I think she trusted the God whom they served. After all, how could two men protect her from an entire city? How could two men shield her from the wrath of her king?

That's something *only God could do* and she believed he would do it.

When Rahab placed the scarlet cord in her window, it was tangible proof for all the world to see that she trusted God to take care of her. When the Israelites captured the city, Rahab was there waiting for them. That is *so* significant. She knew the invasion was coming, so why didn't she flee? What an incredible testimony to her faith. She made no attempt to escape, no attempt to save herself. Instead, she waited for the Lord to rescue her. And not only her but her entire family as well.

Is there anything in your life that gives evidence you are counting on God, and God alone, to take care of you? Or do you constantly hedge your bets, setting up a contingency plan, just in case God doesn't come through?

Rahab took God at his Word and she was willing to go against the crowd. Rahab believed God and she *did something about it.* Rahab believed God would take care of her, and refused to waste time developing a contingency plan. She had total God-confidence. Do you? If we want to be remembered as women of faith, we would do well to follow in the footsteps of Rahab, the role model.

1. Name four reasons why Rahab is a model of faith for us.

2. Do you take God at his Word? Do you believe he will do what he says he will do? How does your life show evidence of that belief?

3. Do you believe God will take care of you? Or do you try to escape difficult situations on your own or at least have a contingency plan? Again, give a specific example of an area in your life where you are completely dependent on God to take care of you.

4. Are you willing to go against the crowd if God calls you to? Give a specific example of something you've chosen to do, which involved/involves going against the crowd.

5. Does your faith translate into action? How?

6. What key lesson did you glean from today's study?

To recap:

- Like Rahab, we must be willing to take God at his Word.
- We must be willing to go against the crowd.
- If we believe God we have to do something about it!
- Our lives should demonstrate (at least in *some way*) that we are relying on God alone to take care of us.

Day Four

You Can Count On God; He Will Never Cast You Out

But Joshua spared Rahab the prostitute, with her family and all who belonged to her, because she hid the men Joshua had sent as spies to Jericho—and she lives among the Israelites to this day.   Joshua 6:25

I love paper plates. I use them, then I throw them out. They serve my needs, then they are out of sight, out of mind. I don't have to bother about cleaning them up. Don't have to worry about what other people might think if they see dirty dishes sitting around my house. I don't have any special feelings toward my paper plates. I don't cherish them. If they tear or crack, I don't try to repair them—I mean, we're not talking Lenox china here. But I keep them around because they are convenient for me to use.

Have you ever felt like a paper plate? Maybe your parents were divorced when you were a little girl and when your father remarried, he cast you aside in favor of his new family. Maybe he moved thousands of miles away and never even bothered with you anymore. Maybe you became a low priority when your new stepdad moved in, bringing his own children along. Or maybe it was when your mom and her new husband had a child "of their own" that you began feeling cast aside.

Have you ever been used? Have you ever experienced that awful feeling that seeps down into the very fiber of your being, when you realize another human being has used you for his own purposes? And when he was done with you, when he got what he wanted, he threw you out. He turned his back and walked away. I know that's a feeling many women have experienced, especially in their relationships with men. And sadly, the men who used them have often been their own fathers. For these women, learning to trust God as a father is a life-long challenge. Let me tell you about my friend Martha. One of Martha's earliest childhood memories is of her grandfather leading her into a dark basement. She can still remember the terrifying look in his eyes. She can still remember the storm cellar doors being shut behind her and she was enveloped in the darkness. She still remembers the fear and the filth, and although God has protected her mind from recalling the details, she knows. . . . She knows she was used and cast aside.

Martha also remembers her four brothers, each in turn, using her. She remembers being led down to the basement, to the dirty laundry pile. She remembers what she was forced to do, and the nickels and quarters she was paid to do it. In her heart, she knows she was used and cast aside.

Although it is incomprehensible to Martha now, she followed the pattern virtually all incest victims follow: she became a promiscuous teenager. By thirteen, she was sleeping with any boy who would have her. By the time she graduated from high school, she had lost count of her partners. She can remember staring up at the ceilings of seedy hotels and in the backseats of cars—and that awful feeling afterward. Of being used and cast aside.

When Martha got married, her husband used his physical strength to force her to perform *the very same acts* she had been forced to perform as a child. When she tried to explain how unthinkable it was to her, he turned a deaf ear. When she hid from the pain by shutting down—by turning frigid as most incest victims do—he forced himself upon her. Time after time, year after year, he beat her and he raped her.

But Martha is learning to trust God, day by day. She's learning the truth of Jesus' words, "All that the Father giveth me shall come to me; and him that cometh to me I will in no wise cast out" (John 6:37, KJV). Do you know what gives Martha hope? Rahab's life is living proof that Jesus' words are true. If there is anyone who deserves to be cast out, it's a prostitute. Prostitutes let people use them and cast them aside *for a living*. Yet when we read Rahab's story, we discover a beautiful, healing truth. Not only did God meet Rahab where she was—in a house of prostitution. Not only did he enable her to become a vessel used for his glory. Not only did he allow her to play a pivotal role in the most glorious military victory in the Old Testament. He wrapped his arms around her and invited her *to go forward with him.*

Our verse for today, Joshua 6:25, tells us that Rahab continued living with the Israelites. She actually became one of God's chosen people. You see, God's plans for Rahab went well beyond accomplishing his objectives. As Jeremiah 29:11 tells us, " 'For I know the plans I have for you,' declares the LORD, 'plans to prosper you and not to harm you, plans to give you hope and a future.' " God didn't just use Rahab and cast her aside. He loved her with an everlasting love. It's the same love he offers Martha, the same love he offers you. God drew Rahab to himself and he promises he will in no wise cast her out. What a beautiful truth. Let's cling to it.

Don't you just *know* that Martha and Rahab will wrap their arms around each other someday in heaven, two kindred spirits? And if you share the pain they carry, you can join them there. Rest assured, my sister, he will in no wise cast you out.

1. What do you learn about God's character from the way he treated Rahab? (i.e. He invited her to live among his chosen people.)

2. Have you ever been used and cast aside? If so, does that experience make it harder for you to trust God?

3. What comfort can you take from the life of Rahab based on today's lesson?

4. What key lesson did you glean from today's study?

To recap:

- No matter what has been done to you in the past, you can trust that God has your best interests in mind.
- If we belong to Jesus, he promises never to cast us aside.

Day Five

God Can Use You, Regardless of Your Past

In the same way, was not even Rahab the prostitute considered righteous for what she did when she gave lodging to the spies and sent them off in a different direction?   James 2:25

Will you dare to believe that God can use you, regardless of the past? When you depend on God alone and walk in God-confidence (rather than self-confidence) there is no limit to what God can accomplish in and through your life. Turn to the very first page of the New Testament and read through Matthew's genealogy of Jesus. See if you find anyone special there. I'll wait for you until you get back.

Well, did you read it? Who is among the women God chose to continue the line of David, to be among the "grandmothers" of Jesus, as it were? None other than Rahab the prostitute. Can we even conceive of what an incredible honor that is? Don't think for one minute that Rahab turned up by accident. God chose her to be part of Christ's genealogy as a lesson to us, that his ways are not our ways. It reminds us that he can choose the most unlikely vessels to accomplish his purposes—yes, even the greatest purpose in the history of human civilization. God knew before the foundation of the world that Christ would come, and he knew that Rahab would be one of the women chosen to bring him. The dream of every Jewish woman throughout history was to be part of the Messiah's line. Yet God granted that privilege to Rahab, a Gentile, a prostitute.

What an encouragement Rahab's life is to us. She stands as an eternal testament to God's grace and mercy. She reminds us that it doesn't matter where you've been. It doesn't matter what mistakes you've made. If you will turn your heart to God, you can become a vessel God can use.

Well, I got so excited about Rahab that I decided to see where else her name turned up. Guess what? She's included in the Great Hall of Faith. Yep, she's in there with the giants—the big boys—like Abraham and Jacob, and Moses and David. It says in Hebrews 11:31, "By faith the prostitute Rahab, because she welcomed the spies, was not killed with those who were disobedient."

But wait: why does the Bible keep calling her Rahab the prostitute? I've got to tell you, for a while it really bugged me. Okay, the girl made a mistake, can we forget about it already? I mean, hey, Moses and David were both *murderers*. Isn't that worse than being a prostitute? Why aren't they labeled? *Why is Rahab labeled?*

I think there are at least two reasons. First, the label reminds us of Rahab's weakness; it reminds us of where she was when God called her. It reminds us, once more, that God often chooses the most unlikely people to accomplish his purposes and bring glory to himself.

Second, I think Rahab is labeled because the Bible is *realistic.* Think about it. We know that she continued living with the Israelites. You can bet that the Israelites knew exactly who she was and exactly what she had been. Even though she obviously settled down and married a nice Jewish man, named Salmon (Matthew 1:5), something tells me there *were certain women who never let her forget.* Do you know what I'm talking about? Maybe you have people in your life who know what you used to be and they never let *you* forget.

When I was a little girl, my brother returned from Vietnam addicted to heroine. Within a few months, drugs had spread through our family like wildfire. When two of my brothers were arrested, it made front-page news in the local paper—and no one in that small town would let us forget. For reasons I couldn't possibly understand, we had been labeled. *I had been labeled.* Drug-addict family.

I can remember the children in my class mocking me—drawing pictures of me and my family with needles in our arms. One day when the teacher stepped out of the room, all of my classmates formed a circle around me and sang "Drug-addict family, drug-addict family" until I ran away in tears. I know what it feels like to be labeled.

Do you know what's ironic? After seeing the human carnage, the wreckage of drugs—after watching drugs destroy my family and rob

51

me of my childhood—guess what I became? I not only became a drug addict, to support my habit I even became a *drug dealer*. Somewhere in my heart of hearts, I believed I was destined to become part of the "drug-addict family," and that chant became for me a self-fulfilling prophecy. Isn't that incomprehensible? Yet, it demonstrates the *power of labels*. You see, old labels don't have to control our future, but if we let them, they can do incredible damage. That's why we have to be so careful how we label our children. We also have to guard against the labels other people—teachers, classmates, neighbors, relatives—place upon them.

Rahab bore a painful label—one that was, no doubt, very difficult to shake. I have a picture in my mind of a group of Hebrew women washing clothes along the river. They are chatting merrily, when along comes Rahab. Suddenly, there is silence. The Hebrew women look at one another. Rahab walks on, alone, to a solitary place farther down and sets about her work quietly. Whispers follow. She knows, at least she suspects, who they are talking about and what they are saying. Maybe not. Maybe those Hebrew women were made of different stuff than women today. I doubt it, though.

And even if they did let her forget, do you think Rahab ever forgot? Can you imagine the things she had done and the things she had witnessed in her life as a prostitute? Do you think that living with the Israelites was enough to drive out those horrible memories? No, I don't think so.

Again, a picture of Rahab comes to mind. This time, she is lying on her bed at night. Her husband, Salmon, and her young son, Boaz, are fast asleep. But sleep won't visit her tonight. The memories are coming back again, like a flood. This is always the hardest time of the day, this darkness, this lying in bed. She tosses and turns, she shakes her head and unconsciously puts her arms in the air. Trying to push away the memory, trying to push away this stranger in the dark. She pleads with God to erase each memory, she pleads with him to free her from those awful places that haunt her in the night.

Do you know what that's like? Are there things you have done and places you have been that *haunt you in the night*? I remember one particular house I used to go to where everyone hung out, buying, selling, and doing drugs. It was unspeakably filthy. The guy who owned the apartment had a tarantula and a boa constrictor that he let roam the place. I can remember nights in a drug-induced daze, staring at the most horrible images, images I wouldn't dare describe on these pages. One of the worst was the night I overdosed on drugs and alcohol and nearly died.

Those days and nights *haunt me*. Even though I am not that person anymore, even though I don't deserve the label "drug-addict" because of what God has done for me in Christ—sometimes the memories still haunt me. I am also haunted by things I have said, words I wish I could take back. Not just the big things that happened long ago, but recent ones, like last Thursday night at a women's fellowship meeting or yesterday's phone conversation. I regret things I've said to my daughter, arguments I've had with my neighbors, bitter words I've allowed to spring from the anger deep within my soul. But one thing Rahab has taught me and I hope she will teach you, too:

Don't let what you used to be prevent you from becoming who you ought to be.

Have you been labeled? Maybe because of something you've done or just because people can be so cruel. Maybe a parent or a teacher or children in the neighborhood put a label on you that you can't seem to shake. Suzie Stupid. Lori the Loser. Fat Phyllis. Or maybe it's something more recent. Maybe you feel like you've blown it too many times: in your marriage, in your neighborhood, at your job, at your church. They've labeled you a *lousy Christian*, and frankly, you feel like the label fits. You've got to let it go!

Like Rahab, we can't let what we used to be prevent us from becoming who we ought to be. How do we know Rahab didn't let that label hold her back? Well, look at the incredible young man she raised. That tells us something about how she must have lived her life before him. Read the book of Ruth and observe the *character and the integrity of Boaz*. Any mother would be proud to call him her own. From now on, when you hear someone talk about Rahab the prostitute, I hope you'll join me in saying, "Oh, you mean Rahab, the great mom? You mean Rahab, the grandmother of Jesus? The one who's commended as a giant of the faith? I can't wait to meet her!"

Will you dare to believe God can use you, regardless of the past? When you depend on God alone and walk in God-confidence (rather than self-confidence) there is no limit to what God can accomplish in and through your life.

1. What is the significance of Rahab's inclusion in the Great Hall of Faith? How does it affect your view of who God is—and who can become a vessel he can use?

2. List all of the negative or destructive labels you currently wear. Try to recall where the label came from and how it has affected your life.

3. How would your life be different if you could let go of that label(s)? If it is a label you "deserve" because of sin in your life, confess and repent, knowing that God stands ready to forgive (1 John 1:8–9).

4. What key lesson did you glean from today's study?

5. What was "This Week's Focus"?

To recap:

- We all wear labels that help or hinder God's work in our lives.
- Don't let what you used to be prevent you from becoming who you ought to be.

Week Three: Knowing

This Week's Focus:

Getting to Know Your Potter

This Week's Focus Verse:

Who among the gods is like you, O LORD?
Who is like you—majestic in holiness,
awesome in glory, working wonders?
In your unfailing love you will lead the people
you have redeemed.

Exodus 15:11, 13

Day One

The Majesty of Our God

There is no one like the God of Jeshurun, who rides on the heavens to help you and on the clouds in his majesty. The eternal God is your refuge, and underneath are the everlasting arms.
Deuteronomy 33:26–27

There's no such thing as a vessel God can't do without. Did you ever think of that? There's not a human being on earth God needs. Sometimes I think we imagine God as a nervous baseball coach, sitting on the sidelines during the ninth inning—pacing the dugout helplessly, wringing his hands and hoping his team can pull off a last-minute victory. Nothing could be further from the truth! He knows the end from the beginning. When we behold his majesty, we realize the victory is assured. We realize he is fully capable of ordering the universe without our assistance.

Doesn't that take the pressure off? You don't have to perform for God. His eternal plan does not hinge on your ability to hit a home run with two strikes against you. Yes, he invites you to become a vessel used for his glory, but that doesn't mean *you* have to figure out a way to bring him glory. He is quite capable of bringing glory to himself, thank you very much. When you understand who the potter is, when you understand the power and majesty of the God you serve, you will realize how little you need to *do*—and how much you need to *yield*, how much you need to *trust*, how much you need to humbly *obey*.

What's even more beautiful is that, when you do blow it (and we all blow it sometimes), he comes to the rescue. He "rides on the heavens to help you." With his "everlasting arms" he stands ready to catch you. The very one who "rides on the clouds in his majesty" is the one who bends down to pick up the broken pieces of your life. He's the very one who gently glues the pieces back together and returns you to a place of being a vessel he can use. He has redeemed you and because you know you are redeemed, you can rest in the promise that he *will lead you*. Even when you can't see where you're going, even when nothing in your life makes sense, you can entrust yourself to your majestic God, knowing that "in his unfailing love, he will lead the people he has redeemed."

For the next two days, let's simply meditate on *who our Potter is. Let's take time to sit at his feet in awe as we behold his majesty.* As you read through the passages for today and tomorrow, note in the margins: (1) the characteristics of God you discover (what is he like, what has he done), (2) what our response should be.

Love the LORD your God and keep his requirements, his decrees, his laws and his commands always. Remember today that your children were not the ones who saw and experienced the discipline of the LORD your God: his majesty, his mighty hand, his outstretched arm; the signs he performed and the things he did in the heart of Egypt, both to Pharaoh king of Egypt and to his whole country; what he did to the Egyptian army, to its horses and chariots, how he overwhelmed them with the waters of the Red Sea as they were pursuing you, and how the LORD brought lasting ruin on them. It was not your children who saw what he did for you in the desert until you arrived at this place, and what he did to Dathan and Abiram, sons of Eliab the Reubenite, when the earth opened its mouth right in the middle of all Israel and swallowed them up with their households, their tents and every living thing that belonged to them. But it was your own eyes that saw all these great things the LORD has done.

Observe therefore all the commands I am giving you today, so that you may have the strength to go in and take over the land that you are crossing the Jordan to possess, and so that you may live long in the land that the LORD swore to your forefathers to give to them and their descendants, a land flowing with milk and honey. Deuteronomy 11:1–9

Yours, O LORD, is the greatness and the power and the glory and the majesty and the splendor, for everything in heaven and earth is yours. Yours, O LORD, is the kingdom; you are exalted as head over all. 1 Chronicles 29:11

> The LORD reigns, he is robed in majesty;
> the LORD is robed in majesty
> and is armed with strength.
> The world is firmly established;
> it cannot be moved.   Psalm 93:1

1. What has been your attitude toward God? Toward learning his Word and spending time in prayer? Has it been a sense of duty? Or have you truly taken delight *in his presence?* Examine your heart before him.

2. How can reflecting on the majesty and goodness of our God inspire you to want *to know him more?*

3. Which verses were most meaningful to you? Why?

4. Write a prayer of response to your awesome God. Thank him for granting you the incredible privilege of spending time in his presence.

5. What key lesson did you glean from today's study?

To recap:

- Our God is an awesome God!
- When we behold the majesty and goodness of our God, it should inspire us to want to know him more.

Day Two

The All-Sufficiency of Our God

H ave you ever met someone famous? Wasn't it neat to feel like
you almost knew him? When we worked at the Billy Graham
Crusade, I was privileged to go down to the stadium floor as a counselor. Lucky for me, the person I was assigned to talk with was determined to get as close to the great evangelist as she could. And,
well, I had to follow her. What an incredible moment when we
inched our way to within yards of Dr. Graham. I stood in absolute
awe as he bowed his head to pray.

Another time, I attended a seminar of a famous Christian writer
and experienced similar awe in her presence. Here was a giant of the
faith, a truly godly woman who had earned the right to be heard. Her
message inspired my heart. Indeed, the impact of her words pulsate
throughout the pages of this book. This illustrious author indicated
she would be available after the seminar to autograph books. I remember thinking, "Wow, I'll actually get to talk to her. Perhaps I'll
have the privilege of really *connecting* with her." However, when I
tried to approach her on a personal level, she gave me (and everyone
else) the proverbial cold shoulder. Ouch! No matter how impressive
these super-Christians are, they are just fellow creatures, not the
Creator.

Isn't it wonderful to know God will never give us the cold shoulder? We can approach the very throne of the God of the Universe.
As his children, we walk into his presence with full confidence,
knowing he will receive us with loving, open arms. *How can we not
delight in that? How can we list that on our "things to do today" as if
we needed to be reminded? Is this real to you?* If we really understood
the character of our God, we would *run to him. Like a child, we would
skip and hop to him.* Instead of running to God, we often run to people. The truth is, even the most noble person will fail us; even the

most well-intentioned, spiritual friend doesn't possess the wisdom and character of God. The next time you face a crisis, remember: you can take it to the throne or to the phone! Which will you choose?

I remember taking my daughter, Leah, to Disneyland. When she saw a performer dressed up like Beauty (from *Beauty and the Beast*), she was overjoyed. I thought she was going to leap out of her skin. Now think about it: she could not contain her excitement in the presence of a twenty-something girl dressed up like a fictional, animated character. *But we don't even bother going to God. And when we do, we can barely stay awake.* What's wrong with this picture?

Now turn to your Bible and take time to study and reflect upon God's character through *the ultimate passage*, Isaiah 40, guaranteed to bless your socks off—or your money back!

Among other things, I hope you noted the following truths about who God is:

- *Eternal, unchanging.* "The word of our God stands forever" (v. 8).
- *Sovereign.* "The sovereign LORD comes with power, and his arm rules for him" (v. 10). He has all power and authority in heaven and on earth.
- *Tender.* "He gathers the lambs in his arms and carries them close to his heart; he gently leads those that have young" (v. 11).

As we behold God's power and majesty, it becomes abundantly clear: God does not need you or me or anyone else. He chooses to give us the privilege of joining him in his work. I can't prove this, of course, but I feel certain God uses frail humans just to prove a point in the heavenlies. Sometimes I can almost see him up there, giving the old side elbow to the angel Gabriel and whispering, "Watch this." (Chuckles all around.) Anyone can win the game with a team of All-Stars, but God demonstrates his power and wisdom by sending in the bench-warmers, the bat-boys, the players no one else would choose. (Christ has already won the ultimate victory, but many battles remain to be fought on earth.)

Take evangelism, for example. God could get the job done much quicker and easier by sending angels. Here's how it would work. Legions of angels would visit a different city each day. They would blast trumpets, shine radiantly, sing gloriously, and proclaim the Gospel flawlessly. How many folks do you think would respond to *that kind* of altar call? Pretty high percentage, I'd bet. I love Billy Graham as much as anyone. In fact, hearing him preach in person was one of the highlights of my Christian life. But something tells me the angels would be much more effective.

Here's another scenario God could use. That is, if efficiency, effectiveness, and the qualifications of the messenger were the key issues. He could send Jesus back down to earth, let's say, once a year. On these occasions, he would come in full glory and splendor. He would proclaim, "I'm God, you're not. Worship me. *Now.*" I'm telling you: This would work, people! And so much easier than all this tediousness of trying to get the message out through human vessels.

Why doesn't God work that way? Is it possible these brilliant ideas never occurred to him? Get real! He's God. He knew about these superior strategies before time began. Clearly, God is *not* interested in the most efficient or effective way of accomplishing his work in this world. Did you ever stop to think of that? What he is profoundly interested in is *you*. And me. And the billions of people who inhabit this earth. He is profoundly interested in molding and shaping us—conforming us to the image of his Son. He is profoundly interested in preparing us for the coming Kingdom, when we will reign as joint heirs with the Son.

Take time to ponder this. It will radically change your idea of what it takes to be qualified as a vessel God can use.

1. Is there any circumstance you face right now which God is not capable of delivering you from? Write the "correct" answer, then write what you really believe, as demonstrated by your attitude and actions.

2. What are some reasons God may be allowing you to remain in your current circumstances? What might he be trying to teach you?

3. What key lesson did you glean from today's study?

To recap:

- God's character demonstrates that he *does not need* us, yet he chooses to accomplish his purposes through our lives.
- God is *able* to deliver us from any circumstance. If he allows us to remain in a trial, it's because he wants us to learn from it.

Day Three

The Longing of Our God

Let's think back to the beginning of human history. God had created the universe and filled it with every living creature. It was a place of beauty and perfection, so why did he spoil it by placing Adam and Eve in the midst? What motivated God to pick up a pile of clay and fashion it into a man? Why did God make man in the first place? He wanted to fellowship with us. He longs to have a deep, personal relationship with each of his children and it grieves him when we turn away. Consider how Jesus agonized over the city of Jerusalem:

> O Jerusalem, Jerusalem, you who kill the prophets and stone those sent to you, how often I have longed to gather your children together, as a hen gathers her chicks under her wings, but you were not willing. Matthew 23:37

Yes, it is God who longs for us, *but we are not willing.* We are not willing to take time to get to know him. Not willing to invest time in his word. Not willing to talk with him in prayer. Not willing to walk with him in daily obedience. Have you ever stopped to consider how much your indifference grieves the heart of God?

How would you feel if the one you loved ignored you? Never called home? Never wrote you letters? How would you feel if the one you love most *treated you exactly the way you treat God?* Let me say that again: How would you feel if the one you love most treated you exactly the way you treat God? If you love God, be willing to show him. He longs for you.

Have you ever longed for someone? Maybe when you were separated from someone special for months, perhaps because of war? Remember when you first fell in love, how you longed for your sweetheart? How even a day apart seemed unbearable? That's the way God

64

feels about you. Can you imagine that? He *longs for you.*

Do you long for God? If not, who or what do you long for? Do you long for wealth, comfort, security, romance, beauty, excitement? Again, if you do not long for God, who or what do you long for? Ponder that question and meditate on what it says about your true heart condition.

1. What do Jesus' words in Matthew 23:37 tell us about his feelings toward his children?

2. Do you honestly believe that God longs *for you?* What do you think that really means?

3. Would Christ say of you, "She was not willing"? In what ways are you not willing to sustain your side of the love relationship with God?

4. Do you long for someone or something more than God? Who/ What is it? No doubt that longing is the very thing preventing you from sustaining your side of the love relationship. Take time now to come before God in a spirit of confession and repentance. Ask him to give you a heart that longs for him.

5. What key lesson did you glean from today's study?

To recap:

- God longs to fellowship with us.
- The major hindrance to that fellowship is that we are not willing.

Day Four

God Reveals Himself Through His Word

Now that you've caught a glimpse of who your potter is, I hope your approach to learning more about him through his word has been transformed. As long as we come to scripture out of a sense of duty or as part of a self-improvement program, we're trying to draw water from the desert. It's only as we realize the incredible privilege we have been given—the right to be called *children of God*—that we can even begin to take joy in his Word.

For the next two days, we're going to get very practical. I realize that this material will be review for many of you, but if it sparks a new idea or two it will be time well spent. If you want to become a vessel God can use, you must come to know and trust your potter. The place to cultivate that relationship is on your knees and in his Word. At a very minimum, every Christian who has the incredible privilege of owning a copy of the Bible (most people throughout the world and throughout history have not had that privilege) should read through it once a year. For "all Scripture is God-breathed and is useful for teaching, rebuking, correcting and training in righteousness, so that the man of God may be thoroughly equipped for every good work" (2 Timothy 3:16–17).

To stay on track, purchase a set of twelve blank index tabs and divide your Bible into twelve equal parts. Mark the tabs January through December. The tabs serve as a visual reminder of where you need to be and when. If you choose tabs with removable labels, you can rearrange your reading program every year. When you sit down to read each day, count forward five pages and insert your bookmark there. You'll automatically know when you've read your allotted portion.

Remember, the number of pages you need to read may be slightly different. For example, if your Bible has study notes, or very small or large print, you may have to read more or less than five pages per day. You can calculate it quite easily:

Divide the total number of pages in your Bible by 365 for the number of pages to read per day.

In addition to your daily read-through-the-Bible program, you should spend time digging deeper into God's Word.

If you are ready for heavy-duty "spiritual meat," try the Precept-Upon-Precept inductive Bible studies. (Precept Ministries was founded by well-known author and speaker Kay Arthur.) Brace yourself for thirty minutes of intense homework five days per week. The studies usually last twelve to twenty weeks, and (at least in my experience) the drop-out rate is quite high. However, the rewards far outweigh the sacrifices. Precept is not for the faint of heart. It *is* for women who are serious about knowing God's Word. Send for a catalog and for information on the Precept study nearest you:

Precept Ministries
P.O. Box 182218
Chattanooga, TN 37422
(615) 892–6814

When I'm not actively involved in a formal study, I use the Quiet Time Worksheet (see page 70). You might use it with your read-through-the-Bible program. You can photocopy the form or write your answers in a notebook to create your own Bible study journal. Whether you join a group or work on your own, the key is to dig in and dig deeper.

Here is God's promise to you, if you will take delight in knowing him through his Word:

Blessed is the [woman]
    who does not walk in the counsel of the wicked
        or stand in the way of sinners
            or sit in the seat of mockers
But [her] delight is in the law of the Lord,
    and on his law [she] meditates day and night.
[She] is like a tree planted by streams of water,
    which yields its fruit in season
        and whose leaf does not wither
Whatever [she] does prospers.   Psalm 1:1–3

Notice the progression in those verses. First you're just walking by a tempting situation; then it gets your attention, so you stop and stand to take a closer look. Next thing you know, you're sitting down with mockers. Sounds like the lure of the television, doesn't it? You're walking through the family room and a show catches your eye. You stand to watch it for a few minutes and the next thing you know you're plopped down on the couch. Four hours later, you've got a mind full of mush. Instead, you could have devoted that time to meditating on God's Word! If you want your ministry to be fruitful, if you want to be a vessel God can use, then stay in his Word. As you do, he will reveal more and more of himself, his will, and his ways to you. Through his Word, you will learn to hear his voice. Know your Potter!

1. List three things God tells us not to do, if we want to be blessed.

2. Examine your life: are you walking, standing, or sitting somewhere you shouldn't? Be specific.

3. What does God promise to the woman who meditates on his Word?

4. How much time do you now spend each day in God's Word? If you answered "no time" or "very little," what is preventing you from investing more time? Jot down some ideas to help you overcome the obstacles that have stood in your way in the past.

5. What key lesson did you glean from today's study?

To recap:

- God has revealed himself through his Word.
- If we truly want to know him, then we should devote the time needed to study his Word.
- God's blessing is upon those who delight in his law, and meditate upon it day and night.

Quiet Time Worksheet

All Scripture is God-breathed and is useful for teaching, rebuking, correcting and training in righteousness, so that the man of God may be thoroughly equipped for every good work.

2 Timothy 3:16–17

Date: _____

Passage: _____

1. Summarize in a few sentences what the passage is about:

2. Is there an example for me to follow?

3. Is there an error I need to avoid?

4. Is there a command for me to obey?

5. Is there a sin I need to forsake?

6. What application of this passage can I make today?

Day Five

Keep God's Word in Your Heart

How can a young [woman] keep [her] way pure?
  By living according to your word.
I seek you with all my heart;
  do not let me stray from your commands.
I have hidden your word in my heart
  that I might not sin against you.
I meditate on your precepts
  and consider your ways.
I delight in your decrees;
  I will not neglect your word.   Psalm 119:9–11, 15–16

In order to be a usable vessel, you must not only get into God's Word, it must *get into you*. Otherwise, how can God direct you to those who need to know him or those who need his comfort? Unfortunately, the New Age gurus and Eastern mystics have given meditation a bad name. When we think of meditation, we think of chanting "ummmmm" with our legs crossed, trying to drive away bad Karma.

Nevertheless, meditation is an important tool for molding us into the kind of vessel God can use. Does that mean God can't use us unless we're graduated with honors from *Evangelism Explosion*? Not at all, God can use whomever he chooses. But the more we do to equip ourselves for service, the more usable we will be in the Potter's hands.

Before we can meditate on God's Word, we must first hide it in our hearts. That's what scripture memorization is all about. In 1992, the Billy Graham Crusade came to Philadelphia. My husband and I participated in counselor training, which involved eight weekly sessions and extensive Scripture memorization. I can remember few other times in our marriage when we were so united in purpose. We'd be sitting at the dinner table, and my husband would cite the reference and expect me to recite the verse. He made it look so easy. My husband can memorize Scripture almost effortlessly. Not only that, he actually *remembers* the verses years later. It drives me nuts!

Well, there's nothing like a little friendly competition to get me going. The only way I could keep up with him was to carry the verses with me constantly. I wrote out each verse on five or six index cards. Everywhere I looked, there were Bible verses. They were in my coat, my purse, my pants' pockets. I tucked them in my Bible, stuck them on shelves and on the kitchen counter. They were in the car, on my desk, and even under my pillow. My husband thought our house had been invaded by an army of index cards.

It sounds crazy and it looks messy, but it works. People often select verses related to evangelism, but don't limit yourself. Memorize Scriptures that will help you overcome specific temptations or to ward off the blues. Memorize Scriptures you can speak to your children or husband as words of encouragement.

Memorizing Scripture offers so many benefits. Most important, it helps to keep our thoughts pure. I don't know about you, but that's a real battleground for me. When I fill my mind with Scripture, there's less room for all the other junk I've usually got hanging around up there.

A memory bank of Scripture also makes us more spiritually sensitive, which means other women will seek our counsel. That way we'll have something productive to do, rather than moping around wallowing in self-pity. I've battled depression since early childhood. And I've discovered that nothing can lift me out of the mire faster than helping someone else.

Plus, when you know Scripture, you can have God-confidence in the face of demonic attacks. When Satan tempted Jesus in the wilderness (Matthew 4:1–11), Jesus responded with confidence. He *knew* what God had said. Don't be duped like Eve, who fell for Satan's oldest line: "Did God really say. . . ?" (Genesis 3:1) Remember, Satan is the Father of Lies and the only way to cut through his lies is with the Truth. Jesus said, "You shall know the truth and the truth will set you free." He also said, "I *am* the . . . Truth." Know the Word and know your Lord!

Several years ago, I was listening to a Chuck Swindoll sermon over the radio while driving in my car. The program was so excellent, I pulled over and jotted down his outline for Scripture memory. You guessed it: on an index card. I'm an index card-aholic and I hope you'll become one, too. Here's what I wrote:

Scripture Memory—Memorize, Personalize, Analyze

1. Set aside fifteen minutes per day for Scripture memory.
2. Choose verses that address your weaknesses. That way, you'll have a vested interest in remembering them.
3. Read the passage aloud over and over.
4. Break the verse down into logical parts. Learn one phrase, then two, until you've memorized the entire passage.
5. Repeat the reference often. (How many times have you searched for a verse in your Bible, murmuring that spaghetti sauce motto "It's in there"? If you can't find it, it's not much good. Learn the reference.)
6. It's better to learn a few verses really well, than many, poorly.
7. Underline difficult terms or key words. Look them up in the dictionary, a concordance, or Bible reference book.
8. Write out the verse from memory. This is a critical step. Something about putting pen to paper makes the words more permanent.

Thanks, Pastor Swindoll!

Here's a strategy I use that sounds crazy—but I promise it works! I write out the first initial of every word in the verse, while looking at the passage. I set it down for a while. When I return, I try to complete the words from memory. Repeat this process several times and you'll be amazed to discover you remember that verse *years* later.

Another very effective—and very painless—way to memorize Scripture is with Scripture songs. Many modern praise songs are scripture set to music. As you sing along, God's Word is making its way into your heart. Ask your local Christian bookstore owner to direct you to cassette tapes or CDs. If you have young children, try Steve Green's *Hide 'em in Your Heart*. It's a big hit at the Partow house, especially with Mom and Dad. If you don't have young children, order it through the mail. No one has to know you listen to preschool tapes all day long.

Whether you use memory cards, Scripture songs, or some other method, do hide God's Word in your heart. God has promised that when we face temptation, he will make a way of escape for us (1 Corinthians 10:13). Often, a Scripture passage is the key that opens the door to freedom. I say carry as many keys as you can.

Throughout this week, we have focused on getting to know the Potter. We looked at his majesty and realized there is no such thing as a vessel God can't do without. That takes the pressure off of us to "perform." We studied his all-sufficiency and found rest in the knowledge that his eternal plans do not depend on us, but rather, he delights in working through our lives. Then we caught a glimpse of God's longing and came to the incredible realization that he yearns for fellowship with us. The only hindrance to that fellowship is that we are not willing.

For the past two days, we have taken a very practical look at strategies for getting to know God's Word, that we may get to know our Potter in a deeper way. Do you want to become a vessel God can use? Then make it your lifelong ambition to know your Potter.

1. How can a woman keep her way pure? (Hint: It's not *by watching soap operas and trashy talk shows!*)

2. What's the best way to face down temptation—to prevent sin from reigning in our lives?

3. Can you think of a recent occasion when calling to mind a passage of scripture might have helped?

4. Can you recall a recent occasion when you have seen the positive effect of God's Word getting into you? If you can't think of an example, what does that tell you?

5. What areas do you most struggle with? Use a concordance to look up appropriate verses to memorize. List them below, then transfer them onto index cards or Post-It™ notes.

6. Write out the eight steps to memorizing scripture:

7. If you've had trouble memorizing scripture in the past, what hindered you? Jot down a few ways that you plan to overcome those obstacles. (Hint: An accountability partner works wonders!)

8. What key lesson did you glean from today's study?

9. What was "This Week's Focus"?

To recap:

- It's not enough to get into God's Word; you have to let God's Word *get into you.*
- An ongoing scripture memorization system is one of the best ways to ensure you are equipped to go wherever and whenever God directs.

Week Four: Accepting

This Week's Focus:

Accepting the Unique Way God Made You

This Week's Focus Verse:

Therefore, if anyone is in Christ, he is a new creation; the old has gone, the new has come! All this is from God, who reconciled us to himself through Christ and gave us the ministry of reconciliation.

2 Corinthians 5:17–18

Day One

You Are a Vessel of Clay

This week's study brings us to the First Requirement for becoming a vessel God can use, which is: "Accepting the unique way God made you." Of course, the surest way to accept who you are is to accept the one who made you. That's why we devoted the first three weeks to laying the foundation of trust. When you realize who your Potter is, how dependable he is, how able he is to use you, it is much easier to accept the way he made you.

Our culture tells us our value is closely linked to the image we see in the mirror. If we're skinny and beautiful, we're valued. But the minute we start tipping that scale above our ideal weight, the minute the force of gravity starts doing its dirty work, *Look out!* The church tells us we have to look great spiritually, otherwise we're a detriment to the cause of Christ—even if God has done a mighty work in our lives.

That's not the way God views us. Did you ever stop to think that God *could easily* have given us incorruptible bodies and morally flawless character? He could have fashioned us out of a material that would never fade, blemish, or blow-it. Instead, he made us out of dirt.

> But we have this treasure in jars of clay to show that this all-surpassing power is from God and not from us.
>
> 2 Corinthians 4:7

Why did God make us out of clay? So that it would be absolutely obvious that anything of eternal value accomplished through our lives is from God and not from us. God created us to bring glory to himself, not glory to ourselves. Over the past several months, God has communicated to me over and over this simple truth: "I will not share my glory with another."

Do we live like we believe we're just jars of clay—unremarkable in every way *except* that the God of the Universe chooses to work through our lives? Oh no, we don't! We try to clean ourselves up, especially when we get around other Christians. We want to look good on the outside. And I'm not just talking about the multi-billion-dollar cosmetic industry! We want to look good spiritually. We want other people to look at us and say, "Wow, what a remarkable woman. What a remarkable Christian."

That's wrong! People should look at us and say, "What a *remarkable God* she must serve. If God can work through an ordinary woman like her, maybe he can work through me, too." God deliberately chose to make us out of clay so that we couldn't steal his glory, but we try to steal it anyway! "We have this treasure in jars of clay, to show that this all-surpassing power is from *God* . . . and not from us."

The woman God can use knows where her value comes from. She is precious because of Who created her. She is valuable because of the One Who dwells within her, not because of the material he used to fashion her or how he chooses to use her.

When I was growing up in the suburbs of Philadelphia, our school would take annual trips to historic sites in the city. We visited the homes of Ben Franklin, Betsy Ross, and other famous patriots. We sat in the very restaurant where the First Continental Congressmen dined. We touched the Liberty Bell. (They let us back then, but don't try it now. You'd probably get arrested!) Throughout the area, private homes had signs proudly touting "George Washington slept here."

Many of these historic sites were remarkably small and dingy. Unless a tour guide had drawn your attention to them, you would certainly pass by without a second glance. They were unremarkable in every way—except one: These humble abodes gained great importance because of the people who had dwelled there.

Remember: The world may pass you by, considering you unremarkable in every way. Yet, if you know Jesus Christ, the very God of the Universe dwells within you through the person of the Holy Spirit. God chose you as his dwelling place and he desires to work through you.

1. What does God have a right to do, according to Romans 9?

2. What is it that makes you valuable?

3. What should people say when they look at our lives?

4. Why is it wrong to want people to say of us, "What a remarkable Christian! I could never be like her?"

5. What key lesson did you glean from today's study?

To recap:

- God is the Potter. He can form us into whatever type of vessel he chooses.
- We are the clay. Our only job is to *yield* to God's work in our lives.

Day Two

Do You Quarrel With Your Maker?

You wouldn't fight with God, would you? Your first reaction is probably, "Well, of course I wouldn't fight with God. I'm no dummy." But what does it mean to quarrel with God? Here's what the Bible says:

> But who are you, O man, to talk back to God? Shall what is formed say to him who formed it, "Why did you make me like this? Does not the potter have the right to make out of the same lump of clay some pottery for noble purposes and some for common use?" Romans 9:20–21

Have you ever stopped to think that every time you compare yourself to someone else, you are quarreling with your Maker? You are saying, "God, you really messed up this time. You didn't make me the right way. You should have made me like so-and-so." Yet, Psalm 139 (and many other passages) clearly demonstrates that God deliberately and carefully created you *exactly the way you are*. He made you to serve and glorify him in a way that *no one else can*. He gave you a unique set of talents, physical characteristics, emotional makeup, temperament, and life experiences *for a specific reason. Until the day you fully accept the package God rolled together on the day he created you, you will never become the woman he intended you to be.*

And now this is a bit trickier: When you pursue a ministry God didn't create you to fulfill—or undertake any project he hasn't called you to—you are quarreling with your maker. You're saying, "God, I've got a better idea than you. I know better than you do what needs to be done around this church. I know better than you do what needs to be accomplished through my life."

Just as the potter fashions a beautiful, delicate vase to grace the table, and a sturdy pot to boil water, God makes different people to fulfill different purposes. There's no factory in heaven; each of us is completely unique. God made you exactly the way he did because he has a specific purpose he wants you to fulfill.

My husband was an art minor in college. I remember watching him work with the potter's wheel. One day, he let me take a shot at it. I'm a cocky kind of person, so I figured it would be easy. I thought I'd just stroll on over, give the wheel a few spins, and *voilè!*, a beautiful vase. I expected the clay to be soft and easy to mold, sort of like a glorified playdough. But it wasn't like that at all. The clay was incredibly heavy. When the wheel was spinning around, I couldn't do anything with the clay. I couldn't believe how hard it was to push and shove. The clay and the force of gravity constantly fought against me. I tried to push it in one direction and it went in the other. That ugly, smelly pile of clay absolutely refused to cooperate.

Sometimes my husband would spend hours working with a pile of clay. He'd finally mold it into a beautiful, nearly complete form. And suddenly, the whole thing would collapse. He'd have no choice but to smash it and start the work all over again. That is, if it hadn't already been reduced to junk-pile material.

You know what? The Bible says *we're just like that pile of clay*. God painstakingly molds and shapes us, preparing us to fulfill a specific purpose. We're almost to the point where we're finally usable, and what do we do? We collapse! We quit studying God's Word, we skip our prayer time, we drop out of fellowship and lose all accountability. Then, God has no choice but to lower the heavenly boom to get us back to center, back to a place where he can begin again, molding us into a vessel he can use.

Oh, how much easier it would be if the clay would cooperate! Oh, how much faster we could become something beautiful if only we would cooperate with the Potter. How much quicker we would be transformed into a useful vessel if only we would stay centered and remain moldable in the potter's hands.

Do you want to know what I quarrel with God about? I think that since I'm a *Christian author*, God should have made me the most eternally cheerful and popular woman around. He didn't. . . .

Instead, he has allowed me to wage a lifelong battle with manic-depression. I'm not just talking PMS or an occasional bout with the blues. I have been clinically diagnosed as a severe manic-depressive, caused by an imbalance of the chemical seratonin in the brain. It's a painful and often baffling disease I've fought my entire life. I never thought I would have the courage to write those words on the printed page, but I want to be transparent enough for God to be able to work through me.

There are days when the depression is so oppressive, I can barely move my body. Walking from the bed to the bathroom is an overwhelming and exhausting exercise. (I sometimes joke that I go so low, the only person who can bring me back up is Jacques Cousteau!) Then there are days when I conceive the wildest schemes and believe I can pull them off, regardless of the obstacles. The results are sometimes humorous and occasionally remarkable—but more often, painful and humiliating.

Yes, God can use cheerful, popular women. And as long as he doesn't put too many of them in my neighborhood, I don't really mind that much. But God can even use a woman like me, and it takes a *remarkable God* to do that. As much as I long to be Miss Personality Plus, I am gaining an increasing understanding of why God made me the way he did. I don't enjoy the darkness of depression, but I know that it is precisely *because* I experience life's pain so intensely that God has been able to work through me. I can't touch lives the way Miss Personality can, with cheer and charm. But, it is the deepest desire of my heart that, through these written words, I can make a difference in my own way. So often I've prayed, "Lord, heal me," when what I needed to pray was, "Lord, use me." You see, God has met me in those dark, dark valleys, so I know he can meet you in whatever valley you're walking through today.

What do you quarrel with God about? Could it be the *very thing* God wants to use as a ministry to others? Do you fight against the potter? Do you fuss and squirm and protest every time he tries to make adjustments in your life? Do you collapse when he attempts major changes? Wouldn't your life be much better if you simply cooperated with God's work in your life? So often I pray, "Lord, let me hear it from your lips, so I don't have to learn it the hard way, from life." Some lessons, though, can *only* be taught the hard way! In those cases, I pray, "Lord, help me get the lesson right the first time, so I don't have to suffer through it again!"

How about you? Will you resolve to remain moldable? Will you decide today to cooperate with the Potter, as he seeks to form you into a vessel he can use?

1. What does it mean to quarrel with God?

2. In what way have you quarreled with your Maker?

3. What are five specific aspects of who you are that you have rejected? Will you accept and give them to God to use as he has intended all along?

4. What key lesson did you glean from today's study?

To recap:

- Do not quarrel with your Maker. Accept the person God made you to be.
- Don't compare yourself with anyone else. God made you into exactly the kind of vessel he wanted you to be.

Day Three

You Have Become a New Person

From the moment you encounter Jesus Christ, who you *were* no longer matters. It doesn't matter where you've been or what you've done. All that matters is who you *are* in Him and who you are destined to become. The Bible says if *anyone* is in Christ, she is a new creation, a person reconciled to God, regardless of past mistakes. We find a beautiful illustration of this truth through the life of the unnamed Samaritan woman at the well.

When a Samaritan woman came to draw water, Jesus said to her, "Will you give me a drink?" (His disciples had gone into the town to buy food.)

The Samaritan woman said to him, "You are a Jew and I am a Samaritan woman. How can you ask me for a drink?" (For Jews do not associate with Samaritans.)

Jesus answered her, "If you knew the gift of God and who it is that asks you for a drink, you would have asked him and he would have given you living water."

"Sir," the woman said, "you have nothing to draw with and the well is deep. Where can you get this living water? Are you greater than our father Jacob, who gave us the well and drank from it himself, as did also his sons and his flocks and herds?"

Jesus answered, "Everyone who drinks this water will be thirsty again, but whoever drinks the water I give him will never thirst. Indeed, the water I give him will become in him a spring of water welling up to eternal life."

The woman said to him, "Sir, give me this water so that I won't get thirsty and have to keep coming here to draw water."

He told her, "Go, call your husband and come back."

"I have no husband," she replied.

Jesus said to her, "You are right when you say you have no

husband. The fact is, you have had five husbands, and the man you now have is not your husband. What you have just said is quite true."   John 4:7–18

Let me ask you something: Does this woman strike you as a good candidate to become a vessel God can use? Basing your evaluation *only* on the passage you just read, what would you expect her spiritual future to be? If we're honest, we will probably admit she is not exactly *our* ideal of a woman God can use. That's because we can't see what was happening in her heart. The reason the Samaritan woman is remembered 2,000 years after she encountered Christ is because she became a new person and God did indeed give her a ministry of reconciliation.

Many of the Samaritans from that town believed in him because of the woman's testimony, "He told me everything I ever did." So when the Samaritans came to him, they urged him to stay with them, and he stayed two days. And because of his words many more became believers.
They said to the woman, "We no longer believe just because of what you said; now we have heard for ourselves, and we know that this man really is the Savior of the world."   John 4:39–42

The Samaritan woman didn't have impressive credentials—spiritual, social, or otherwise—but she knew enough to listen to Jesus and to consider his claims upon her life. She didn't pretend to have all the right answers, but she was willing to pose the right questions. And she was willing to point people to Christ so they, too, could make their own decision about his claims. She knew there was nothing within her that would "win people to Christ," nothing she could point to and say, "Hey, don't you want to be like me?"

What did she know? She knew she was a sinner who had met Jesus face-to-face. That was enough to transform her. She knew her past mistakes didn't matter. All that mattered was telling as many people as possible about Jesus. She wasn't a perfect woman, but she was a vessel God could use.

No matter who you are or what mistakes you've made, the most important thing you can know about yourself is whether or not you have encountered Christ. Let's rejoice in the knowledge that Jesus meets us right where we live and accepts us in whatever condition we come. What we did yesterday doesn't matter; it's the future that counts. If you will only believe, God can transform you into a vessel he can use.

1. From a human perspective, what were some of the "strikes" against the Samaritan woman? Why wouldn't she be our ideal of a vessel God can use? Be specific.

2. What is the most important thing any woman can know about herself?

3. At what point does who you *were* no longer matter?

4. What key lesson did you glean from today's study?

To recap:

- The Samaritan woman knew what Jesus had done in her life. She knew spreading that message was the only thing that mattered.
- No matter who you are or what mistakes you've made, the most important thing you can know about yourself is whether or not you have encountered Christ.

Day Four

God Will Transform You From the Inside Out

For I resolved to know nothing while I was with you except Jesus Christ and him crucified. I came to you in weakness and fear, and with much trembling. My message and my preaching were not with wise and persuasive words, but with a demonstration of the Spirit's power, so that your faith might not rest on men's wisdom, but on God's power.   1 Corinthians 2:2–5

Do you want to look good on the outside? Most women do. Cosmetics and cosmetic surgery are multi-billion-dollar industries in America. So much of a woman's identity is caught up in how she looks. Imagine the desperation of a woman who would allow someone to slice open her breast and insert a plastic bag filled with chemicals, believing that somehow, someway, that will bring her the happiness and fulfillment she longs for.

You're probably thinking, "Why is she talking about plastic surgery? I'd never do a thing like that. Well, liposuction, maybe . . ." I'm talking about plastic surgery because that's exactly what many Christian teachers today specialize in. Helping people look good on the outside, ironing out the wrinkles of selfishness, tucking in the fat of sin. To our shame, we've fallen for it. We just want to look good *on the outside of the vessel.* Never mind the inward reality; we want Band-Aids, we want quick fixes.

I'm fed up with "the secret keys," "the 22 ways," and "the surefire plan." I'm fed up with the phony masks of self-styled Christian experts and the dishonesty of those who proclaim one thing while living something completely different. The only reason the church is so disillusioned when these people fall, is because they followed after the persuasiveness of men, rather than looking for a demonstration of the Spirit's power.

With each passing day, I become more determined to know *nothing except Christ and him crucified*. I don't have all the answers. I haven't arrived. I don't have the perfect marriage or the perfect child. I only know that Jesus Christ has done something incredible in my life. I was lost and now I'm found. I was blind and now I see. I used to be at Point A and now I'm at Point C. Hey, it's not Point Z, it's not *nirvana*. But it's forward progress. And the only way I can explain how I got from where I started to where I am now is . . . *the God Thing*.

I may not look perfect on the outside, but I'm changing inside. Nothing magical, but I've lost a pound of sin here and an ounce of crummy attitude there. I may not make the cover of "Super Christian Today," but I'm pressing onward in the faith. My Creator has done what I've termed "the God Thing" in my life. It's something powerful and unexplainable and no one can take it away from me. I blow it every day of my life, but I'm not who I used to be and I'm not who I would have been. I'm clinging to *the God Thing* with both hands, and I'm not letting go until he brings me safely to the other side.

Judging another human being is no business for mere mortals. The truth is, you have no idea how far another person has traveled in her spiritual journey. She may be at Point B, but God may have done *a mighty work in her life* to get her there. She may have experienced heaping doses of the God Thing. In contrast, a woman who appears to have it all together—a woman at Point Q—may have experienced a *very small dose* of the God factor or maybe even none at all. So don't consider her outward appearance. Here's what the Bible says:

> But the LORD said to Samuel, "Do not consider his appearance or his height, for I have rejected him. The LORD does not look at the things man looks at. Man looks at the outward appearance, but the LORD looks at the heart."   1 Samuel 16:7

Isn't that the most wonderful news you've ever heard??
Stop comparing yourself to other people! Stop fussing over the outside of the vessel. Let God transform you from the inside out. Let him perform the God Thing in your life.

1. As a Christian, what do we need *to know*? (1 Corinthians 2:2–5)

2. Define the God Thing.

3. Why shouldn't we judge others—or worry about how they judge us?

4. What does the Bible say God looks at—what are his judgments based on?

5. How large is the God Thing in your life? What point are you at . . . and where did you start?

6. What key lesson did you glean from today's study?

To recap:

- The God Thing is the distance between where you started and where you are today.
- Don't judge others based on outward appearances. You may dramatically underestimate or overestimate the power of what God has done in their lives.
- God looks at the heart—his judgment is based not on where we are, but on how far we've come.

Day Five

Understanding Who You Are in Christ

You're going to feel great when we're done today. I know, because preparing this lesson was the most encouraging exercise I have undertaken in a long time. The Bible has *so much* to say about who we are in Christ and it's all good news. The next time you're tempted to look at another woman and think: "I wish I were as _____ as her," meditate on what tremendous blessings are yours as a daughter of the reigning King. There's no way you can have an inferiority complex with a list of qualifications like the following:

- *Child of God*: "Yet to all who received him, to those who believed in his name, he gave the right to become children of God." John 1:12, and 1 John 3:1 "How great is the love the Father has lavished on us, that we should be called children of God! And that is what we are!"
- *Overcomer*: "For everyone born of God overcomes the world. This is the victory that has overcome the world, even our faith. Who is it that overcomes the world? Only he who believes that Jesus is the Son of God." 1 John 5:4–5
- *New Creation*: "Therefore, if anyone is in Christ, he is a new creation; the old has gone, the new has come!" 2 Corinthians 5:17
- *Minister of Reconciliation*: "All this is from God, who reconciled us to himself through Christ and gave us the ministry of reconciliation: that God was reconciling the world to himself in Christ, not counting men's sins against them. And he has committed to us the message of reconciliation." 2 Corinthians 5:18–19
- *Christ's Ambassador*: "We are therefore Christ's ambassadors, as though God were making his appeal through us." 2 Corinthians 5:20
- *Redeemed*: "You are not your own; you were bought at a price [re-

deemed]. Therefore honor God with your body." 1 Corinthians 6:19–20

- *Seated With Christ in the Heavenly Realms*: "And God raised us up with Christ and seated us with him in the heavenly realms in Christ Jesus, in order that in the coming ages he might show the incomparable riches of his grace, expressed in his kindness to us in Christ Jesus." Ephesians 2:6–7
- *Priest*: "You also, like living stones, are being built into a spiritual house to be a holy priesthood, offering spiritual sacrifices acceptable to God through Jesus Christ." 1 Peter 2:5
- *Foreknown, Predestined, Called, Justified, and Glorified!* (Whew!) "For those God foreknew he also predestined to be conformed to the likeness of his Son, that he might be the firstborn among many brothers. And those he predestined, he also called; those he called, he also justified; those he justified, he also glorified." Romans 8:29–30
- *Heir of God and Co-Heir With Christ*: "Now if we are children, then we are heirs—heirs of God and co-heirs with Christ." Romans 8:17

Let's think about what it means to be heirs of the father: Since God is the King and we are his daughters (co-heirs with Jesus, the Prince of Peace) that makes each and every one of us a *princess*. Cool! Where's my tiara? I've already shared with you one of the labels I wore as a child: drug-addict family. There was a label I longed to wear, but one that always eluded me, somehow. I wanted to be a princess. I wanted to be Daddy's little princess, just as every little girl does.

I remember how the daddy across the street, Mr. Calland, always called his daughter Sharon a princess. (He also read her the Bible and sang "Jesus Loves Me" every night before she went to bed. What a great guy!) How I longed to be cherished as Sharon was. One day I asked Mr. Calland if I could be his princess, too. He said, "No, you are your daddy's princess." "Really?" I asked, surprised to hear the news. "Of course," he said. "Just go ask your daddy. He'll tell you." So I ran home as fast as I could.

It was a Saturday afternoon—a beautiful Indian Summer day. My mom was fixing dinner (I think it was sausage sandwiches . . . that's how vivid this memory is!) and my father was sitting at the kitchen table drinking beer with his buddies, as was his custom most every weekend. I burst into the room and popped the question: "Daddy, am I your princess?" He looked at me in stunned silence, then suddenly threw back his head and howled with laughter. "No! You're maggot mouth and leprosy legs!" (Those were his nicknames for me. Maggot mouth because my teeth had rotted and turned brown, and most were decayed down to stubs. Leprosy legs came from the swelling and bleeding sores of mosquito bites that covered most of my body. We lived in a very humid, mosquito-infested area of New Jersey. I played outside all day long and was fair game for the nasty creatures, to which I was highly allergic.) I still remember the roars of laughter and the fists of drunken men pounding the table. I still remember feeling I'd never be anyone special to my father . . . or anyone else.

I don't share that story to say my dad was an awful guy. In fact, I absolutely adore my father, and now that I am older, I realize that was just his way of teasing. I now know my father meant what he said "in fun" but the pain in my child's heart was just as real. Oh, please, be careful how you label your children! Please be careful about teasing and name-calling. We have banned *all teasing* from our home and I strongly encourage you to do likewise. Yes, it's good for a quick laugh—but at what price?

Teach your children who they are in Christ. And teach yourself while you are at it. Yes, you are a jar of clay, but you contain a heavenly treasure. Yes, you are a jar of clay, but you have been chosen to dwell in the house of the king. Not only that, you've been adopted by the King. You are a *princess*.

Throughout this week, we focused on the importance of accepting the unique purpose for which God fashioned you. We explored what it means to be a jar of clay and the importance of refusing to quarrel with your Maker. We looked at the life of the Samaritan woman at the well, who became a "new person," was used mightily in ministry, thereby fulfilling God's purpose for her life.

We discussed the importance of allowing God to transform you from the inside out, rather than looking for ways to spruce up the outside of the vessel. Today, we reviewed all of the incredible credentials that are ours in Christ. God has created us to be princesses in his household. Accept it and rejoice in it!

The First Requirement for becoming a vessel God can use is:

Accept the way God made you.

1. Which of your "credentials in Christ" is the most meaningful to you? Why? Write a prayer thanking God for it.

2. What key lesson did you glean from today's study?

3. What was "This Week's Focus"?

4. What is the first requirement for becoming a vessel God can use?

To recap:

- Your "credentials" in Christ are incredible.
- You are a princess. Live like one!

Week Five: Emptying

Being Emptied of Self to Make Room for What God Wants to Do In and Through Your Life

This Week's Focus Verse:

Do nothing out of selfish ambition or vain conceit, but in humility consider others better than yourselves. Each of you should look not only to your own interests, but also to the interests of others.

Philippians. 2:3–4

Day One

Christ, Our Example

The Second Requirement for becoming a vessel God can use is: "Being emptied of self to make room for what God wants to do in and through your life." Unfortunately, our lives are too cluttered with selfish pursuits. Indeed, the greatest hindrance we face is self-centered living. Me, my agenda, my ideas, my plans. Here's what the world tells us: Live your life focused on yourself. Be proud of yourself and your accomplishments. Boost your self-confidence any way you can. When you need strength, look to yourself and your own abilities. Turning to God is a "crutch" for the weak. Strive to make yourself look good in the world's eyes and to be a success according to the world's standards.

However, if we want to be used by God, we've got to make a 180-degree turn. We've got to be emptied of our own private agendas and focus entirely on God's agenda. It's called seeking first the Kingdom and it's a whole lot easier said than done. It means placing your confidence in God and God alone. It requires humbling yourself enough to recognize your total dependence on God.

Here's how the Bible puts it:

Do nothing out of selfish ambition or vain conceit, but in humility consider others better than yourselves. Each of you should look not only to your own interests, but also to the interests of others.

Your attitude should be the same as that of Christ Jesus:

Who, being in very nature God, did not consider equality with God something to be grasped, but made himself nothing, taking the very nature of a servant, being made in human likeness.

And being found in appearance as a man, he humbled himself and became obedient to death—even death on a cross!

Therefore God exalted him to the highest place and gave him the name that is above every name, that at the name of Jesus every knee should bow, in heaven and on earth and under the earth, and every tongue confess that Jesus Christ is Lord, to the glory of God the Father.

Therefore, my dear friends, as you have always obeyed—not only in my presence, but now much more in my absence—continue to work out your salvation with fear and trembling, for it is God who works in you to will and to act according to his good purpose.

Do everything without complaining or arguing, so that you may become blameless and pure, children of God without fault in a crooked and depraved generation, in which you shine like stars in the universe.   Philippians 2:3–15

The phrase "made himself nothing" is from the Greek word *kenoo*, which literally means "to make empty" or "to make of no reputation." Just as Christ emptied himself on the cross, so must we be emptied of our private agendas, our hidden longings, our selfish dreams and desires. Often, we're so wrapped up in our own little world, we can't see people drowning around us.

The cartoon here illustrates this point well.

Let me pose a simple question: Who is drowning around you?

Christ was never so preoccupied with himself that he ignored those drowning around him. Even as he hung on the cross, his concern was for the men hanging next to him, for the people who had condemned him, and for you and me.

Even during his torturous death, he wasn't looking out for himself; he was looking out for us. In short, he emptied himself. If we want to become vessels God can use, the very first step is to be emptied. It's really basic when you think about it: There is simply no room for God to work in a life that's already full of itself. There's no room for the blessings he wants to pour into us.

Begin today, emptying yourself to make room for what God wants to do in your life. Set aside time to meditate on the following prayer, which beautifully illustrates how we can imitate Christ in our daily life. May it become the heartfelt prayer of your life.

Seventeenth-Century Nun's Prayer

Lord, you know better than I know myself that I am growing older and will someday be old. Keep me from the fatal habit of thinking I must say something on every subject and on every occasion. Release me from the craving to straighten out everybody's affairs. Make me thoughtful, but not moody. Helpful, but not bossy. With my vast store of wisdom, it seems a pity not to use it all, but you know, Lord, that I want a few friends at the end.

Keep my mind free from the endless recital of details; give me wings to get to the point. Seal my lips on my aches and pains. They are increasing, and love of rehearsing them is becoming sweeter as the years go by. I dare not ask for grace enough to enjoy the tales of others' pains, but help me to endure them with patience.

I dare not ask for improved memory, but for a growing humility and a lessening cocksureness when my memory seems to clash with the memories of others. Teach me the glorious lesson that occasionally—I may be mistaken.

Keep me reasonably sweet. I do not want to be a saint—some of them are so hard to live with. But a sour old person is one of the crowning works of the devil. Give me the ability to see good things in unexpected places, and talents in unexpected people. And give me, Lord, the grace to tell them so.   Amen.

1. Christ gave us a pattern to follow, in terms of "emptying himself."

From the Philippians passage, list as many things as you can that you must be emptied of:

2. "Your attitude should be like that of Christ Jesus"—describe that attitude. Be specific:

3. In what way are you like the dog in the cartoon? So wrapped up in your own concerns that you disregard people drowning all around you?

4. List people who are drowning. What specific help can you bring to them?

5. Using the *Seventeenth-Century Nun's Prayer* as a model, write out your own prayer expressing the character qualities you long to possess when you reach the end of this life's journey.

6. What key lesson did you glean from today's study?

To recap:

- Christ is our example: He emptied himself. We must be emptied of our hidden agendas, our secret longings, our wants and demands.
- Open your eyes to the people "drowning" all around you.
- Let it be your prayer to daily be conformed more and more to the character of Christ.

Day Two

The Christlike Life

From the Philippians 2:3–15 passage we introduced yesterday, we can glean five key ingredients for the life that is truly Christlike—a life that is "emptied of self."

Stay focused on God and his agenda, rather than yourself and your own convenience. If Christ were interested in his own comfort, or the convenience of life's here-and-now, he never would have gone to the cross. Recall Jesus' plea in the Garden of Gethsemane: "Going a little farther, he fell with his face to the ground and prayed, 'My Father, if it is possible, may this cup be taken from me. Yet not as I will, but as you will' " (Matthew 26:39). He went to the cross because he stayed focused on God's eternal agenda.

We find an incredible contrast *in the very next verse*. Watch what the disciples are up to: "Then he returned to his disciples and found them sleeping. 'Could you men not keep watch with me for one hour?' he asked Peter" (Matthew 26:40). What were they focused on? God's agenda? No way! Their only concern was their own comfort and convenience. What a lesson to us.

Remember what the apostle Paul wrote: "For our light and momentary troubles are achieving for us an eternal glory that far outweighs them all. So we fix our eyes not on what is seen, but on what is unseen. For what is seen is temporary, but what is unseen is eternal" (2 Corinthians 4:17).

Cultivate an attitude of thankfulness. Here's the secret to doing "everything without arguing or complaining." If you really want to be emptied of yourself, so you can enjoy maximum effectiveness in ministry, there's no more vital step than this. Rather than demanding *more* from God, realize that you don't deserve even one of the blessings he has already given you. Why not make a list of everything you have to be thankful for?

You can transfer the list into your Bible and read it daily. It will absolutely transform you. Make a fresh list the next time your joy goes AWOL. Just sit down and start writing from memory. It's amazing how humbling this experience is. I started my "Thankful List" in 1982 and now have 127 major blessings that I've traced over the years. From this list, I've compiled my Top 20 blessings on an index card. I review that card every single day. It gives me the attitude adjustment I need when I start feeling full of myself or start making demands.

Treat other people as better and more important than you. Unfortunately, rather than loving and serving people, rather than treating them the way we would want to be treated, we pass judgment. We criticize and condemn. God can't use a woman with a critical spirit! James 4:12 reminds us, "There is only one Lawgiver and Judge, the one who is able to save and destroy. But you—who are you to judge your neighbor?" We've got to be humble enough—we've got to be so emptied of ourselves—that we can admit we don't know the full story. We can't possibly know all that a person has gone through or how far they've come. Why not? Because we're not God. We *may act like we think we're God, but we're not God.*

Live your life in an attitude of prayer. The apostles had no time for prayer; they were too busy sleeping and resting. Sound familiar? It sure does to me! The only way *we* can discern the Father's will is how *Jesus* discerned the Father's will: through prayer. And not just the dinnertime send-up or the good-night, sleep-tight variety prayer. First Thessalonians 5:16–18 instructs us to "Be joyful always; pray continually; give thanks in all circumstances, for this is God's will for you in Christ Jesus."

Earnestly desire to be used by God, rather than to use God. Jesus easily could have used his influence in the heavenlies to get out of going to the cross. He tells his disciples, "Do you think I cannot call on my Father, and he will at once put at my disposal more than twelve legions of angels? But how then would the Scriptures be fulfilled that say it must happen in this way?" (Matthew 26:53–54) Here again, Jesus wasn't about the business of using God for his own convenience. Instead, he was willing to be used by God to fulfill the Scriptures.

Yet how often we try to manipulate God. How often we treat him like a butler. God, do this. God, do that. We hem in our demands from either side with a "Please" and an "Amen" but it's orders, just the same. And the hidden message is: "And if you don't, Lord, I'm outta here so quick you won't know what hit." Even when we are supposedly serving God, what we really want is glory or excitement or a sense of significance. That's wrong! Love him for who he is, not for what he does for you. Not even for the joy he brings, not even for the miracles he performs.

There have been very few occasions in my life when I heard God speak to me in a way that was so clear it was virtually audible. The first time was several days after I became a Christian back in July of 1980. I was walking along the shores of the Delaware River at Camp Tuscarora, Pennsylvania. It was late evening and the moon was absolutely luminous in the night sky. The Lord laid out before me his mission for my life. It was a glorious moment I'll never forget.

The second occasion was anything but glorious. I was facing some trials that had completely robbed me of my joy. I was bitter and angry at God and the world. I was sitting in church one Sunday morning, feeling very sorry for myself and bemoaning my predicament.

Suddenly, I heard an incredibly anguished sobbing. I could feel the pain in my soul and it was overwhelming. Then God whispered to me, with such anguish that I knew I was bringing him tremendous grief, and I'll never forget the words: "What more do you want from me, Donna? What more do you want? I have given you *everything*. I have given you my Son."

Christ emptied himself on the cross for me. He poured out his very life, but I wanted more. I was *so full of myself* that I demanded more. Oh, how we need to empty ourselves, just as Christ did. Oh, how we need to let go of our hidden agendas, our dreams, our demands.

How much fuller can our hearts be? What greater joy can we possibly experience than the joy of knowing that our heavenly Father loved us so much that he gave his only Son, that we might spend eternity with him. We can demand no more; he has already given all. It is enough.

1. What five principles of a Christlike life can we glean from the Philippians passage?

2. In what ways are you—on a daily basis—focused on yourself rather than on God?

3. Who are you living for—God or self? What would happen—on a daily basis—if you actually lived for God?

4. Do you actively cultivate an attitude of thankfulness or are you discontent? If discontent, what changes will you make?

5. Do you maintain a positive view of others, recognizing that only God has the right to judge? Or do you have a critical spirit?

6. Specifically, name one person you are standing in judgment of. What would happen if you let go of being "right" and let God be the judge? Right now, release that person to God.

7. Do you live your life in an attitude of prayer? If not, what changes can you make today?

8. Is your heart's desire to be used by God or do you try to use God to further your own agenda?

9. What have you been demanding from God? Will you resolve to let it go?

10. What key lesson did you glean from today's study?

To recap:

- Focus on God's plan, rather than your private agenda.
- Actively cultivate an attitude of thankfulness.
- Maintain a positive view of others.
- Live your life in an attitude of prayer.
- Earnestly desire to be used by God, rather than to use God.
- God has already given us everything we need: salvation through his Son, Jesus Christ.

Day Three

Letting Go of the Pride of the Past

C hrist is our greatest example of what it means to be emptied of self, but he is not the only example the Scriptures provide. The apostle Paul also spoke of emptying himself—of throwing away everything he thought he had to offer God. And admitting instead that all his accomplishments, all his zeal, and all his knowledge were just a collection of rubbish compared to what Christ had done.

> But whatever was to my profit I now consider loss for the sake of Christ. What is more, I consider everything a loss compared to the surpassing greatness of knowing Christ Jesus my Lord, for whose sake I have lost all things. I consider them rubbish, that I may gain Christ and be found in him, not having a righteousness of my own that comes from the law, but that which is through faith in Christ—the righteousness that comes from God and is by faith. I want to know Christ and the power of his resurrection and the fellowship of sharing in his sufferings, becoming like him in his death, and so, somehow, to attain to the resurrection from the dead.
>
> Not that I have already obtained all this, or have already been made perfect, but I press on to take hold of that for which Christ Jesus took hold of me. Brothers, I do not consider myself yet to have taken hold of it. But one thing I do: Forgetting what is behind and straining toward what is ahead, I press on toward the goal to win the prize for which God has called me heavenward in Christ Jesus.
>
> All of us who are mature should take such a view of things. And if on some point you think differently, that too God will make clear to you. Only let us live up to what we have already attained. Philippians 3:7–16

Paul says he considered his past accomplishments rubbish *so that*

106

he could gain Christ. He says the two things are mutually exclusive. Do you agree? Or do you harbor the idea that you can cling to your worldly credentials and still follow Christ?

Did Paul have a right to be full of himself? Well, according to worldly standards he certainly did. In fact, before he dismisses them as rubbish, Paul himself lists his qualifications to serve God. Look at Philippians 3:4–6:

> Though I myself have reasons for such confidence. If anyone else thinks he has reasons to put confidence in the flesh, I have more: circumcised on the eighth day, of the people of Israel, of the tribe of Benjamin, a Hebrew of Hebrews; in regard to the law, a Pharisee; as for zeal, persecuting the church; as for legalistic righteousness, faultless.

I don't know what your qualifications to serve God include, but it would be pretty tough to match Paul's. Can you trace your ancestry straight back to the tribe of Benjamin? Were you trained as a Pharisee? Are you an expert in the law? Could you faultlessly observe the law for even *a week*? Yet, Paul—this Hebrew of Hebrews, this giant among the apostles, the man who contributed more books to the New Testament than any other man—called it all rubbish. He completely emptied himself and relied on Christ.

Can you honestly say that you consider every strength, every advantage, every accomplishment you have, rubbish? Maybe you were raised in a "good family" like my husband. Maybe you've got blue blood pulsing through your veins. Maybe you've been popular your whole life—homecoming queen and Miss Congeniality all rolled into one. Maybe you know exactly how to win friends and influence people. Maybe you were a straight-A student, attended a high-class prep school and went on to an Ivy League university. Or maybe your good looks and charm enabled you to "marry well."

Maybe, just maybe, you're one of the women who has actually managed to "have it all." You climbed the corporate ladder with ease, raised beautiful, well-balanced children, kept the spark alive in your blissfully happy marriage, while jogging three miles a day and volunteering for charity. *Good for you. Now for the ultimate test:* Can you lay all of that out on the table and call it rubbish?

I didn't start out in life with many advantages. If there's anything pulsing through my veins, it's probably Irish whiskey. If I may quote one of my relatives, "We come from a long line of horse thieves, beer guzzlers, and barroom brawlers. It's a proud tradition." Nevertheless, I have managed to accomplish a thing or two (according to the world's standards). And I just can't bring myself to call those accomplishments rubbish. If you're in the same boat, there's only one explanation. You're still full of yourself. You haven't truly been emptied of self. And as long as self remains, Christ doesn't have all the room in your life that he desires. He doesn't have enough room to fully transform you into a vessel he can use.

Will you wake up one morning and throw away the pride of the past? Will it happen in a magic moment? That has not been my experience! Instead, the process of being emptied of self—including being emptied of the pride of the past—is a lifelong journey. So take it one day at a time.

1. What did Paul say he had to be emptied of? What did he hope to gain?

2. What are you holding on to? What is it that you think you have to offer Christ? Make a list below of everything the world might be impressed with. Include your family background, education, ministry experience, accomplishments, and any other qualifications:

3. Now, can you honestly say that you consider these things rubbish? *Are they nothing but a* total loss *in your eyes?* Take some time to reflect on this:

4. Transfer your "impressive" list onto a separate piece of paper— then tear it to shreds or burn it in a fireproof vessel. If you are completing this study as part of a group, bring your lists with you to the next meeting and destroy them together.

5. What key lesson did you glean from today's study?

To recap:

- You must come to the place of considering even your greatest accomplishments as "rubbish," just as the apostle Paul did.
- Releasing the pride of the past is a lifelong process.

Day Four

Letting Go of the Pain of the Past

In recent years, dredging up the past has become a popular pastime. As someone who could qualify for virtually every 12-step group on the market, I know there is certainly value in understanding our past. However, if we really want to become a vessel God can use, we've got to let go of the pain. We don't let go of the lessons we learned; we don't let go of the ministry opportunities our pain opens up for us; but we do close the wound and let it heal. We don't keep "picking off the scab." Take it from someone who spent many years pickin' scabs—it never brings healing, it only causes more pain.

Let me give you an example of someone who has refused to let the pain of her past control her life. Several years ago, I met a delightful woman when I was speaking at a Christian writer's conference. She told me she wanted to write about her life experiences, and I thought, "Gee, who doesn't? Ho-hum." But when Valerie shared her story with me, I knew it had to be told, far and wide.

About a year later, while I was preparing to speak at a conference on "Becoming a Vessel God Can Use," the Lord kept bringing Valerie to my mind. Then, the week before the conference, Valerie called me "out of the clear blue sky" to tell me how God had used me in her life. She shared with me that, since our meeting, her ministry, called Wounded Warriors, has grown to touch thousands nationwide. Valerie gave me permission to share her story at the conference—and with you on the pages of this book:

> Shortly after we were married, I discovered my husband had an obsession with pornography. He started out bringing home pornographic magazines. About a year later, he began going to the X-rated movie theaters every month or so. Eventually, he progressed to once a week.
>
> All the while, he lived a double life. He played in the music

group at church and would stand up and testify what Jesus was doing in his life . . . then he'd come home and watch porno movies. Women in the church would say, "Oh, you're so lucky to have such a godly husband." They had no idea. . . .

When VCRs became popular, he bought one for the express purpose of watching porno at home. I would put my children in the car and drive around until three o'clock in the morning, just to shield them from the garbage that was being poured into our home.

As time went on, the movies became more explicit and more violent. He would always tell me about them, whether I wanted to hear about it or not. At this point (nine years into our marriage), his addiction had grown from "over-the-counter" magazines to more than fifteen hard-core X-rated movies per week. If I tried to stop him from watching them, he'd become angry and violent. If he did watch them, he'd become perverted and violent. There was no winning. It was sheer insanity.

During this time, he went from a loving husband to a man who physically abused his family, and sexually abused me. Finally, I confronted him. I told him he had to make a choice, because I just couldn't bear the double life anymore. I couldn't bear the lies. I told him to choose between his pornography—or his family and his God.

The next day, he committed suicide.

How does someone like Valerie come to grips with today's lesson? How does she accept that a sovereign God has allowed these painful experiences in her past? This book isn't about theory, it's about reality. So I decided to ask Valerie, point-blank, whether or not she agreed with the principles I have set forth here. Her answer was an unequivocal yes. "It was all worth it, for the ministry I have today to hurting women. I know I'm exactly where God wants me to be, and there's no way I could be here without first living through the pain." Valerie's motto is: "God uses our past to change other people's futures."

So how do we neutralize the power of the past? How can we be so completely *emptied* of the past that it can't control us anymore? There's only one way: Jesus Christ. Tony Campolo has said, "Your past is an excuse for present behavior *until* the day you receive Christ." Stop looking back. Stop looking for explanations. Look to the Potter and be emptied of the past. If you do, he will absolutely astound a watching world with what he can accomplish through your life.

Because Valerie has processed the pain of her past, today she is a beautiful example of a vessel God can use. No doubt, God has allowed you to endure painful trials in your life. The only question is: *What will you do with that pain?* Will you allow it to cleanse you and transform you into a vessel God can use to minister to a hurting world? Or will you let it make you bitter? The choice is entirely yours.

1. What does it mean to let go of the pain of the past?

2. What *shouldn't* we let go of, in terms of past pain?

3. What pain do you need to let go of?

4. How can turning your pain into a ministry to others help you let go of it?

5. What key lesson did you glean from today's study?

To recap:

• Don't let the pain of your past control your future.
• Turn your painful experiences into a ministry to others.

NOTE: You can contact Valerie Martinez, Wounded Warriors, P.O. Box 110464, Nashville, TN 37222 or call (615) 262–5202.

Day Five

Letting Go of Our Hopes for the Future

Brothers, I do not consider myself yet to have taken hold of it. But one thing I do: Forgetting what is behind and straining toward what is ahead, I press on toward the goal to win the prize for which God has called me heavenward in Christ Jesus.

Philippians 3:13–14

All this week, we've looked at the emptying process. We must not only be emptied of the past, but our plans and dreams for the future as well. Notice that Paul's sole focus (in Philippians 3) was heavenward. As he looked into the future, he didn't see beautiful grandchildren, a retirement home in Arizona, an RV to travel the countryside in. No, he saw only his heavenly prize. Can you honestly say that, when you think of the future, the only place that comes to mind is heaven? Can you honestly say that the only rewards you long for are of the heavenly variety? *Take some extra time to really pray over the hopes and dreams you are holding on to. Let God show you what you need to let go of in order to make more room for him.*

Just four days after I wrote this week's lesson, I had the privilege of attending a conference featuring Elisabeth Elliot. Her talk the first evening posed the question: "What are you afraid of?" I'm not a very fearful person, so I had to really ponder for a while. Gradually, almost unconsciously, my hand drifted over my stomach. At four months pregnant, I was surprisingly large; in fact, my mother was sure I was having twins. The thought drifted through my mind, "Nothing could be worse than losing this child." The key verse for the evening was Psalm 16:5: "LORD, you have assigned me my portion and my cup; you have made my lot secure." God gives each of us just the right amount of suffering needed to conform us to the image of his Son.

We returned on Saturday morning to explore the question: "What are you sure of?" Mrs. Elliot talked of God's sovereignty and love. She described how her confidence remained firm, even after the devastating loss of two husbands. At the lunch break, I said to the woman next to me, "You know, it's amazing, I've never really experienced a tragedy. Sure, I've had my share of hassles and hard times, but nothing tragic." Just moments later, I realized I was having a miscarriage.

The past two weeks have been a blur of pain and tears and guilt and prayer, but through it all, God's peace and grace have indeed been sufficient. It's hard to understand why God allows twelve-year-old girls to deliver perfectly healthy babies; while I, a woman married twelve years, cannot. But what am I sure of? I am sure God is in control. I am sure he loves me. I am sure that this, too, will work for my ultimate good. It certainly gave me a powerful illustration of what it means to be "emptied"—to release my hopes and dreams to God's loving and perfect will.

When I returned from the doctor, having received the official word, I ran to my closet and gathered up all my maternity clothes. My husband took them away and banished them to a dark corner of our garage. I realized this, too, was a powerful illustration of the emptying process. I had to *literally* put away my plans to make room for what God wanted to do in and through my life.

During this time, I've found comfort in the words of a Twila Paris song called "A Heart That Knows You." I don't know the details of what she was experiencing when she wrote it, but I do know she was in the midst of the emptying process. She describes so beautifully what it feels like to struggle against what God is doing and finally come to a place of accepting. Accepting that we will never be truly free in Christ until we let go completely, until we embrace his will entirely, until we learn to wait on God's timing rather than demanding things our way *now*.

Even those of us who've followed Christ for many years through hard, hard places are amazed to discover "pockets of resistance" in our hearts. Places where we continue to hold out for what we want, regardless of what God wants.

As God takes you through your own emptying process, I trust you will find the same comfort I have been comforted with: the knowledge that every road we go down, God goes down before us. And every step we take has been appointed from the beginning, either to help us grow or to help us point the way for others.

As 2 Corinthians 1:3–5 says, "Praise be to the God and Father of our Lord Jesus Christ, the Father of compassion and the God of all comfort, who comforts us in all our troubles, so that we can comfort those in any trouble with the comfort we ourselves have received from God. For just as the sufferings of Christ flow over into our lives, so also through Christ our comfort overflows."

Well, we've had a tough week together exploring what it means to be emptied of self. We saw that both Christ and the apostle Paul emptied themselves, and we gleaned important principles from their lives and ministries. We emphasized the importance of releasing both the pride and the pain of the past, while letting go of our hopes and dreams for the future. And why must we let go of all these things? In order to make room for what God wants to do in and through our lives.

The Second Requirement for becoming a vessel God can use is:

Be *emptied* of self to make room for God.

1. Write out your agenda for the future. Include both earthly and heavenly desires. Be honest.

2. Are you willing to let these things go? How would you react if not even one of these dreams comes to pass?

3. Whatever you are holding on to has the potential to cause you much pain. It means you still need to be emptied of self. Write out your prayer that God will continue to turn your eyes toward eternal things.

4. What is your "dearest desire"? Is your heart one that is willing to wait on God for its fulfillment or are you still struggling in his hand? Pray over the matter.

5. What key lesson did you glean from today's study?

6. What was "This Week's Focus"?

7. What are the first two requirements for becoming a vessel God can use?

To recap:

- You must relinquish not only your past but your hopes and dreams for the future.
- Whatever we hold on to can become a source of great pain in our lives.
- God desires for us to comfort others with the comfort we receive from Christ.

Week Six: Cleansing

This Week's Focus:

Allowing God to Cleanse You Even If the Process Is Painful

This Week's Focus Verse:

If we claim to be without sin, we deceive ourselves and the truth is not in us. If we confess our sins, he is faithful and just and will forgive us our sins and purify us from all unrighteousness.

1 John 1:8–9

Day One

Cleaning Staff—God's People

Sorry to tell you this folks, but this week is not going to be much fun. Other than being emptied of yourself, cleansing is the toughest part of your journey to becoming a vessel God can use, especially if God has to break out the heavenly Brillo pad. The Third Requirement for becoming a vessel God can use is "Allowing God to cleanse you even if the process is painful."

I'll tell you right up front: I think this is the very point where many Christians miss it. God does not promise to forgive unconfessed sin. I'll repeat that again: *Nowhere in Scripture does God promise to forgive unconfessed sin*. Indeed, our verse for this week says it all: "If we claim to be without sin, we deceive ourselves and the truth is not in us." Before we can be cleansed, we must confess. However, we can't confess our sins until we confront them, which often requires taking a long hard look in the spiritual mirror.

Unfortunately, sin sometimes has a way of sneaking up on us. We wake up one day and realize we've been wallowing in filth for months. Usually, the wake-up call comes in the form of *reaping consequences*. If we're fortunate enough to have the right people in our lives, the wake-up call can be delivered by a trusted friend. That's what happened to David:

> The LORD sent Nathan to David. When he came to him, he said, "There were two men in a certain town, one rich and the other poor. The rich man had a very large number of sheep and cattle, but the poor man had nothing except one little ewe lamb he had bought. He raised it, and it grew up with him and his children. It shared his food, drank from his cup and even slept in his arms. It was like a daughter to him.
>
> "Now a traveler came to the rich man, but the rich man refrained from taking one of his own sheep or cattle to prepare a

meal for the traveler who had come to him. Instead, he took the ewe lamb that belonged to the poor man and prepared it for the one who had come to him."

David burned with anger against the man and said to Nathan, "As surely as the LORD lives, the man who did this deserves to die! He must pay for that lamb four times over, because he did such a thing and had no pity."

Then Nathan said to David, "You are the man! This is what the LORD, the God of Israel, says: 'I anointed you king over Israel, and I delivered you from the hand of Saul. I gave your master's house to you, and your master's wives into your arms. I gave you the house of Israel and Judah. And if all this had been too little, I would have given you even more. Why did you despise the word of the LORD by doing what is evil in his eyes? You struck down Uriah the Hittite with the sword and took his wife to be your own. You killed him with the sword of the Ammonites. Now, therefore, the sword will never depart from your house, because you despised me and took the wife of Uriah the Hittite to be your own.'

"This is what the LORD says: 'Out of your own household I am going to bring calamity upon you. Before your very eyes I will take your wives and give them to one who is close to you, and he will lie with your wives in broad daylight. You did it in secret, but I will do this thing in broad daylight before all Israel.' "

Then David said to Nathan, "I have sinned against the LORD."

· Nathan replied, "The LORD has taken away your sin. You are not going to die. But because by doing this you have made the enemies of the LORD show utter contempt, the son born to you will die." 2 Samuel 12:1–14

What courage it took for Nathan to confront the King of Israel, especially because David was quick to anger and even quicker to use his sword. Nathan cared enough to confront, even when the stakes were high. More to the point, Nathan was the vessel God used to bring David back to his senses. Let me ask you this: When is the last time someone looked you in the eye and said, "*You* are the woman!" When is the last time someone clearly articulated a specific sin in your life and challenged you to repent? Unless you attend a very unusual church or are part of an extremely devoted small group, I've got a feeling the answer is "Not lately," and your answer very well could be "Never."

If that's the case, only one of three possibilities is true:

(1) You are sinless, so there's nothing to confront. But since the Bible says that is humanly impossible ("For all have sinned and fall short of the glory of God," Romans 3:23), let's consider another option.

(2) You are a remarkably talented hypocrite, so no one suspects your sins, which you do in private. Hmmm, now there's a possibility. But, I seem to recall, Jesus didn't have many nice things to say about hypocrites: "Woe to you, teachers of the law and Pharisees, you hypocrites! You are like whitewashed tombs, which look beautiful on the outside but on the inside are full of dead men's bones and everything unclean" (Matthew 23:27).

(3) No one knows enough about your life or cares enough about you, to be willing to play a role in drawing you closer to Christ. Door #3 sounds like the winner (well, actually the loser) to me.

I suspect one of the reasons the body of Christ in America today is so lukewarm and ineffective is because we don't dare confront one another with the truth. People with the gift of prophecy—the ability to "see" what God is doing in the lives of individuals and the church and speak it forth—are despised. No one wants to hear the insights God has laid on their hearts; they'd rather hear something *encouraging*.

Why am I saying so much about prophets? Because God has placed prophets in your path. Think of people who "cut right to the chase," who seem to "look right through you," who say things that make you uncomfortable. Those are the prophets. If you are serious about allowing God to cleanse you, don't push them away. Rather, invite them into your life.

We all need a Nathan—someone who will confront us with the truth. We won't always *like* what the prophet has to say, but if we want to become a vessel God can use, we must be continually cleansed. That requires confession and repentance. And that requires confronting the sin in your life. And sometimes that requires a friend to hold the mirror of truth before you. If you don't have such a friend, *get one.*

1. What did Nathan confront David about?

2. Do you think it was easy for Nathan to confront David? Why or why not?

3. Can you think of anyone you know who may have the gift of prophesy? Reflect back on things they've said that offended you. Pray about whether or not they had indeed confronted you with the truth. Indeed, virtually all criticism contains at least a nugget of truth.

4. Everyone needs at least one Nathan in her life. If you have such a person, thank her for the important role she plays in your life. If not, find such a person. Give her permission to get close enough to know your sin and to confront you with it. *Do it today.*

5. What key lesson did you glean from today's study?

To recap:

- God uses people, especially prophets, to draw our attention to unconfessed sin.
- Do not despise the prophets in your life. Welcome those people who dare to confront you with your sin.

Day Two

Cleaning Tools—Prayer and Meditation

Lately, I've been reading anything I can get my hands on by Andrew Murray, a South African pastor and missionary born in 1828. Bethany House Publishers has updated Murray's timeless classics to make them more accessible to the modern reader. There are thirteen books in the Andrew Murray Christian Maturity Library, including *The Believer's Absolute Surrender, The Believer's Call to Commitment,* and *The Believer's Secret of Holiness.* There's also the Andrew Murray Prayer Library (four books) and the Andrew Murray Devotional Library, with five books including *The Believer's Secret of Waiting on God,* which is the gem I'm currently reading.

Here's an excerpt:

> The great lack of our Christianity today is, *we do not know God.* The answer to every complaint of weakness and failure, the message to every congregation or convention seeking instruction on holiness, should simply be: *Where is your God?* If you really believe in God, he will put it all right. God is willing and able by his Holy Spirit. Stop expecting the solution from yourself, or the answer from anything there is in man, and simply yield yourself completely to God to work in you. . . .
>
> Pray to God that we might get some right conception of what influence could be made by a life spent, not in thought, or imagination, or effort, but in the power of the Holy Spirit, wholly waiting upon God [i.e. meditation] (p. 14).

To this I would merely add: waiting upon God *for cleansing.* When we come before God in prayer, let's not bring a list with us. So often, we are only concerned with our needs and wants and demands. Instead, let us focus entirely on him. Let's enter his presence and keep quiet, allowing him to reveal himself to us in a new and personal way.

How will that help the cleansing process? Simply this: the more we see God for who he is—the more we behold his holiness—the more we will see our *need of cleansing*. It is inevitable. If we were to encounter God as Isaiah did, we would have the same reaction:

> "Woe to me!" I cried. "I am ruined! For I am a man of unclean lips, and I live among a people of unclean lips, and my eyes have seen the King, the LORD Almighty."   Isaiah 6:5

When you meet with God in prayer and he continues to reveal more of himself to you, holiness will be the natural outgrowth. Here's a test you can take to see whether or not you are allowing the Holy Spirit to do his work of cleansing in your life:

What specific sin did the Holy Spirit convict you of this past week? What specific thing did you do or say—or fail to do or say—that the Holy Spirit revealed you needed to repent of? I would like to suggest to you that if you don't have an answer it *ain't 'cause you didn't sin*. It's because you are not allowing the Holy Spirit the time he needs to convict and cleanse you of sin.

What better passage of Scripture to meditate on for cleansing than Psalm 51. It is no coincidence that these are the very words David wrote after the prophet Nathan confronted David with his adultery. Once we have confronted our sin—or been confronted with it—the cleansing process can begin. We will keep the lesson short today, so you can take time, *right now*, to bring your sins before the Father. Allow your heart to soak in the words of David. Don't rush; there is nothing you need to do today that is more important than allowing God to cleanse you.

> Have mercy on me, O God, according to your unfailing love;
>   according to your great compassion blot out my
>   transgressions.
> Wash away all my iniquity and cleanse me from my sin.
> For I know my transgressions, and my sin is always before me.
> Against you, you only, have I sinned and done what is evil in
>   your sight, so that you are proved right when you speak
>   and justified when you judge.
> Surely I have been a sinner from birth, sinful from the time
>   my mother conceived me.

Surely you desire truth in the inner parts; you teach me
wisdom in the inmost place.
Cleanse me with hyssop, and I will be clean; wash me, and I
will be whiter than snow.
Let me hear joy and gladness; let the bones you have crushed
rejoice.
Hide your face from my sins and blot out all my iniquity.
Create in me a pure heart, O God, and renew a steadfast
spirit within me.
Do not cast me from your presence or take your Holy Spirit
from me.
Restore to me the joy of your salvation and grant me a willing
spirit, to sustain me.
Then I will teach transgressors your ways, and sinners will
turn back to you.
Save me from bloodguilt, O God, the God who saves me, and
my tongue will sing of your righteousness.
O Lord, open my lips, and my mouth will declare your praise.
You do not delight in sacrifice, or I would bring it; you do not
take pleasure in burnt offerings.
The sacrifices of God are a broken spirit; a broken and
contrite heart, O God, you will not despise.

Psalm 51:1–17

1. Note any significant thoughts that came to mind as you meditated
   upon Psalm 51.

2. Did the Holy Spirit bring to mind any specific sins you need to
   be cleansed of? If so, write a prayer of confession and repentance.
   If not, spend more time in prayer!

3. Is your prayer life making a difference in your daily life? How so? If not, is it possible that the reason prayer doesn't change you is because you are focused on self, rather than God?

4. What key lesson did you glean from today's study?

To recap:

- Prayer and meditation upon God's words are vital to the cleansing process.
- When we confess our sins, God will give us a clean heart and a renewed spirit.
- If the Holy Spirit has not recently convicted you of sin, it's not because you haven't sinned! It's because you are not allowing him to cleanse you.

Day Three

The Cleansing Process—Trials

There is no oil without squeezing the olives,
no wine without pressing the grapes,
no fragrance without crushing the flowers,
and no real *joy* without sorrow.
Pack Up Your Gloomies In a Great Big Box
by Barbara Johnson

Here's the Donna Partow version of an otherwise unpleasant verse: "Consider it pure joy, my sisters, whenever your husband takes you out to dinner and a movie, or whenever you win a free shopping spree at Nieman Marcus." Okay, those of you who *really* know your Bibles well probably already suspect that verse isn't in there. Although we've got to admit, a lot of times we *live* like we believe that's what the Bible teaches.

No, the Bible says, "Consider it pure joy, my brothers, whenever you face trials of many kinds, because you know that the testing of your faith develops perseverance. Perseverance must finish its work so that you may be mature and complete, not lacking anything." Ah, now we're getting down to the nitty-gritty of this cleansing process and it ain't pretty.

Let's take a closer look at the "so that" stuff. It says we have to endure *all kinds of tough times, so that* we can become mature and complete, not lacking anything. See, the problem is we like that part about "not lacking anything." And we've made fools of ourselves enough times to realize that being "mature and complete" might keep us out of a fix or two. But you can't get one without the other. You can't grow and mature without enduring tough times. It's a package deal. Two for the price of one.

Just out of curiosity, how many of you would prefer that shopping spree at Nieman Marcus? Are you ready for a really outlandish statement: Every woman reading this book has led the absolute *perfect life!* You lucky girls! You had the perfect parents, the perfect childhood, you lived in the perfect neighborhood and attended the perfect schools. You grew up and married the perfect husband or remained perfectly, blissfully single.

It's true. You have led the perfect life—for you. God has given you *exactly, precisely, perfectly,* the life experiences you need to become a vessel he can use. God knew *exactly* what he was doing every step of your life. Let's be clear about one thing, though: God does not condone sin; he didn't cause your heartaches and he does not rejoice in your pain. But in his sovereignty, he allows it.

Nor does he delight in your foibles and failures, but in his mercy he redeems them, using them to move you forward in the journey. As a vessel handmade by God and chosen for his service, you can be confident that he will use every circumstance—even those you "bring upon yourself"—to bring you closer to the image of his son. "And we know that in all things God works for the good of those who love him, who have been called according to his purpose" (Romans 8:28).

Not long ago, I had lunch with a fellow Christian author Margie Erbe. A number of years ago, she nearly died from a brain hemorrhage and God miraculously healed her. She wrote a book about her ordeal called *My Joy Came in the Morning.*[1] As a result, she was invited to share her testimony around the world. She was on *The 700 Club* with Pat Robertson. She even had an audience with the Pope.

Then she received an invitation to speak at Campus Crusade for Christ's Arrowhead Ranch in California. The Lord spoke to her very clearly about this event, telling her it would be a pivotal moment in her life. So she decided to invite her entire family along to enjoy this special occasion. She gave her testimony and all went well. Afterward, her thirteen-year-old son, Danny, congratulated her saying, "You were wonderful, Mom, and you looked so pretty." A few hours later, he was in a roller-blading accident and died.

It is impossible for us mere mortals to understand why God allows such unspeakable suffering to enter our lives. And we're on

---

[1]To order *My Joy Came in the Morning* ($8.50) or her latest book on the loss of her son, *I Miss You So* ($8.50), contact: Margie Erbe, P.O. Box 39364, Phoenix, AZ 85069.

shaky ground when we start offering up our own explanations, as did Job's so-called friends. Yet one thing is clear: the Bible says we are to consider such trials to be pure joy, knowing they are conforming us into the image of Christ.

Indeed, the only way we can survive with our sanity and our faith intact is to refuse to demand an explanation from God. The moment we start functioning in the realm of "why," we're in the danger zone. The only safe and sane questions to ask are: "What now, Lord?" "Where do you want me to go from here?" and "How can I take this pain and use it to minister to others?" God is in the redemption business. When we turn our pain over to him, he redeems it and turns it into something good.

Are you convinced that you have led the absolute *perfect life . . . for you?* God knew exactly what he was doing, every step of your life. Nothing—no experience, however painful—will be wasted in God's economy.

How do trials cleanse us and move us closer to becoming a vessel God can use? Here's how Andrew Murray puts it:

> In time of trouble say,
> First, he brought me here. It is by his will I am in this place;
>   in that will I rest.
> Next, he will keep me in his love and give me grace in this
>   trial to behave as his child.
> Then, he will make the trial a blessing, teaching me the
>   lessons he means me to learn, and working in me the
>   grace he intends for me.
> Last, in his good time, he can bring me out again, how and
>   when only he knows.
> Say, I am here:
> By God's appointment,
> In God's keeping,
> Under his training,
> For his time.
>
> —from *Humility*

You are reading these pages today for a reason. It is by God's appointment; you are in his keeping and under his training, for his time. Isn't that exciting? More to the point, *the trials* you are facing now—

and the trials you have lived through—have been allowed by a loving God *for a specific reason.*

The only way suffering can cleanse, rather than destroy us, is if we yield our dreams and agendas to his will. Again, it comes back to understanding who God is and who we are. He is the Potter and we are the clay. He has an eternal plan that our finite minds couldn't possibly conceive. We can't know all the answers. But we can make a decision. Ask yourself now: "Am I willing to allow God to mold me and shape me—using whatever tools, whatever circumstances he chooses?" If you can answer yes, then you can become a vessel God can use.

1. Why can we say that every Christian has lived the perfect life . . . for her?

2. Is there anything in your past that seems far from perfect? Are you beginning to sense that even the hard things were part of God's perfect plan for you?

3. Are there some "Why's" you haven't been able to release—some questions that God must answer *before* you fully yield yourself to him? List them below and resolve to let go.

4. When have you seen God use trials in your life to bring about Christlikeness?

5. What key lesson did you glean from today's study?

To recap:

- When suffering comes—as it surely will—our survival depends upon releasing the "Why's" and asking instead, "What now, Lord?"
- One of the most important questions you can ask yourself is this: "Am I willing to allow God to mold me and shape me—using whatever tools, whatever circumstances he chooses?"

Day Four

The Cleansing Work of Silence

I have been avoiding this "Week Six, Day Four" for many months, not sure how to approach the subject of silence. You see, I'm a noisemaker from way back. Not exactly the silent type. Just this morning, I joined in a discussion on some ways that we can open ourselves up to the leading of the Holy Spirit. Just for fun (and in hopes someone might come up with a brilliant idea I could "borrow") I suggested silence. You know, turning off the TV. Turning off idle phone conversations. Turning off meaningless chit-chat. When I got to the idea of turning off the radio, even Christian radio, shock waves swept through the room. One man responded: "I think it's a personal choice. I think each person has to decide. Silence isn't good for everybody. When it's too quiet, my mind goes in the wrong direction." There were approving nods around the room.

Now, you'll be very proud of me, because I *did not* tell him what I'm about to tell you. (Hey, I actually managed to keep silent! It's a miracle!) His mind did not go in the "wrong direction," it went in the right direction—even if it went straight to the gutter. His mind went exactly where his heart wanted to go. And if he doesn't deal with the underlying matters of his heart, his mind will continue to follow the wrong path. And it may only be a matter of time before his body joins the parade. By surrounding himself with noise—even if it's the noise of Christian music—he is simply avoiding the real issue.

Keep silent. Listen to your heart. Hear what it is saying to you about who you really are and what you really desire. Now, I didn't say follow your heart, because your heart will often lead you astray. I simply said, turn off the noise and listen to what is really going on inside you. Then, once you have confronted the truth, God can cleanse you. But as long as you are denying that you've got a dirty heart, God cannot begin the work of cleansing.

Don't be afraid of silence. Don't let the world deafen you to the truth about your heart's true condition. If the silence reveals the sin in your heart, confess it. Repent of it. Ask God to cleanse you of it. Silence is your partner in the process of cleansing. If it reveals dirt, it is doing exactly what it is intended to do.

Let me rephrase that:

If silence reveals sin in your heart, it is doing exactly what it is intended to do.

I first began thinking about this issue after a conversation with my close friend, Mariette Holland. She served with the Gray Nuns of the Cross for fifteen years and said the value of silence was the most important lesson she learned. Her husband, Dr. Jerry Holland, is a former Augustinian monk who lived in a monastery for 30 years. I asked them to share their insights on silence with me and they wrote me a beautiful letter. With their permission, I want to share their reflections with you:

"The Gift and Power of Silence"

Mariette and I share a treasure few couples have experienced. We each lived with a daily gift called the *magnum filentim*, which is Latin for "the great silence." Each evening from the conclusion of night prayers and chapel until after breakfast and morning mass, we were given the privilege of hours of silence. We were able to spend time in solitude and contemplation, time to reflect on our higher purpose in life, time to indulge ourselves in our four human endowments: self-awareness, conscience, imagination, and independent will.

All those years we spent in silence gave us the strength and direction we never would have received otherwise. You do not find direction by traveling, but by standing still and listening to the sounds of silence. The early Christians did not go into the desert to escape people, but to learn how to serve them better.

Sadly, I have found that people today are quite wary of silence; they find it to be a tiresome burden or a deprivation. They fear it. They do everything they can to escape it.

Mariette and I no longer have the discipline of the *magnum filentim* and we miss it. But there are lots of times when we consciously turn off the radio and the TV and go about our lives in self-imposed solitude. We walk around the lake in the morning in silence, drinking in the hues and colors of the sky reflected in the water. We genuinely *listen* to the sounds of the ducks, and the breeze as it caresses the trees. And we find strength in that silence.

In one of our training sessions, we urge people to find their secret garden, their place of quiet and solace. To escape to it and restore their souls on a regular basis. Most participants find it very difficult to do; they sneak communication with one another; they fall asleep; they are embarrassed by their need for noise. But those few who give themselves unstintingly to the solitude that lies deep within themselves are amazed at the strength it brings them.

Are you avoiding silence . . . or are you cultivating it? Jesus actively pursued it: he often withdrew from the crowds and encouraged his disciples to do likewise. We, too, must learn to be still. He still says to each of us: "Come with me by yourselves to a quiet place and get some rest" (Mark 6:31).

Do you feel compelled to surround yourself with noise? Can you leave off the radio in the car or in the kitchen? Could you turn off the ubiquitous TV for a day or a week or a month or forever? We recently put our TV in the closet for a month and it was sheer heaven. My husband begged me to bring it back out, but even he had to admit, the peace in our home was magnified a million times by the silence.

Have you ever considered a *quiet vacation* or quiet recreation? Standing in line at Disneyland, filling our kids with "memories," is not the only way. If the truth were told, what we and our children need is an outlet for what we've already stored. We need to empty out the garbage. We need to process the good. We don't need to fill our lives with more stuff, more activities, more clothes, more, more, more.

Even idle conversation and, in our home, bickering is a way of driving away the silence. Often noise is our way of covering up. It's our way of avoiding deeper questions and concerns of the heart. The pain of the past, the demands of today, the fear of the future.

Why not institute a quiet hour in your home? Even if the children are too old for an afternoon nap, you can still require them to remain quietly in their rooms—reading, reflecting, resting—for an hour each day.

Ironically, even our quiet times are noisy—that is, busy with activity. Checking off Bible reading charts, working our way through prayer lists, studying devotional guides. Is there any room for quiet in your Quiet Time? I'm guilty of it, too. As the writer of this study, I've felt compelled to give you something to *do* each day. Well, not today! For today, just be *quiet*. Don't reflect on anything in particular. Don't jot anything down. Don't work through your list of prayer requests. Just sit quietly and listen to your heart.

1. Sit quietly and listen to your heart.

To recap:

- Our modern culture drives us to fill our lives with noise. We need to take time, each day and each week, to empty it all out.
- In the silence, we find out where our heart is.
- If silence reveals sin in our hearts, it is doing precisely what it is intended to do: confess the sin and ask God to cleanse you.

Day Five

The Cleansing Effect of Spiritual Disciplines

During this past week, we have explored a variety of ways that God uses to cleanse us, including:

- God's people
- Prayer and meditation of his Word
- Trials
- Silence

Each of these tools the Potter can use in your life, but not when you resist him. Not when you slip away from his loving hands. Not when you fuss and squirm so much you end up crashing to the floor. You see, there is a balance, even a tension here—as in every aspect of our existence—between God's sovereignty and man's responsibility. Yes, God has a master plan for conforming us to the image of his Son. Yes, he desires purity and holiness in our inward parts. Yes, he sovereignly works all things together for our good so that we can say with confidence, "I have led the perfect life . . . for me."

At the same time, a seemingly contradictory principle holds equally true. We are responsible for the choices we make. Not only that, we are guaranteed to reap the consequences of every foolish decision, each careless act. How do we reconcile these two principles? Frankly, no mere mortal can fathom this mystery. It's like trying to comprehend the Trinity or how Jesus could be both fully God and fully man. If we are honest, we admit it is impossible. Nevertheless, we know by faith that God is three-in-one. We know that Jesus was the God-man. And we know by faith that God's sovereignty and man's responsibility stand together. Here's an approach that has helped me and perhaps will help you too:

137

> *Act assuming you are fully responsible:*
> *Trust and pray knowing God*
> *is fully sovereign over the outcome.*

So how do you apply this to the cleansing process? Let's look at some examples:

- God will sovereignly send his people into your life with words to spark your growth . . . but your responsibility is to be available and willing to hear their words with an open heart.
- The God of the Universe will communicate with you through prayer, sovereignly leading you along the path he has marked out for you . . . but you are responsible for setting aside time in prayer.
- God will teach you through the Bible, sovereignly customizing the lesson to suit the student's needs . . . but it is your responsibility to study and meditate upon his Word.
- God will allow painful trials to enter your life, trials that are filtered through loving hands and sovereignly designed for your ultimate good . . . but it is your responsibility to learn the lessons God intends and to "behave as his child." (Otherwise, God repeats the lesson!)
- God will cleanse you in the silent moments, speaking in his still, small voice . . . but you have to turn off the noise and listen.

Throughout this study, we have said, "Don't worry about the outside of the vessel; focus on the inward reality and let God take care of appearances." But just because we're not *focusing* on outward appearances doesn't mean that the inward reality won't become more and more obvious to a watching world. Quite the contrary. Devoting ourselves to cultivating the spiritual disciplines is tangible evidence that we are committed to cooperating with the Holy Spirit in the work of cleansing. As we allow God to transform us from the inside out, as he works the miraculous God Thing in our hearts, our lives will harvest an increasing bounty of righteousness—love, joy, peace, patience, kindness, faithfulness, gentleness, and self-control.

The Third Requirement for becoming a vessel God can use is:

Allow God to *cleanse* you, even if the process is painful.

1. List each of the spiritual disciplines discussed in today's study; then note to what extent you are cooperating with the Holy Spirit by cultivating the disciplines of personal holiness.

2. What key lesson did you glean from today's study?

3. What was "This Week's Focus"?

4. What are the first three requirements for becoming a vessel God can use?

To recap:

- God uses a variety of tools to cleanse us, but it is our responsibility to cooperate with him in the process.
- Act, assuming you are fully responsible; trust and pray, knowing God is fully sovereign over the outcome.

Week Seven: Filling

Being Filled and Constantly Refilled With the Living Water of God's Spirit

This Week's Focus Verse:

Be filled with the Spirit. Speak to one another with psalms, hymns and spiritual songs. Sing and make music in your heart to the Lord, always giving thanks to God the Father for everything, in the name of our Lord Jesus Christ.

Ephesians 5:18–20

Day One

Filled With Living Water

God created us as empty vessels, designed to be filled *only* with him. All of us sense that emptiness inside—that "God-shaped void"—and we are driven to fill it. We can try to fill it with a career, with money, with a beautifully decorated house, with the right clothes and makeup and hairstyle. We can try to fill it with food, with housecleaning, with church busywork. The possibilities are endless. However, if you want to become a vessel God can use, the Fourth Requirement is "Being filled and constantly refilled with the Living Water of God's Spirit." It is not enough to fill ourselves with doctrines and principles, traditions, rituals, and habits. We need the Living Water that flows from the Throne of God into the lives of those who abide in him—then through their lives to quench the thirst of a parched and dying people.

Jeremiah 2:13 describes it this way: "My people have committed two sins: They have forsaken me, the spring of living water, and have dug their own cisterns, broken cisterns that cannot hold water." Rather than turning to the source we try to satisfy ourselves with things that can never satisfy.

You may recall a certain Samaritan woman who knew all about that. (We met her during Week 3.) She tried to fill her life with men. She went from relationship to relationship seeking the fulfillment that only God can give. Then she encountered Jesus.

He looked past her mistakes and made her a promise: "Everyone who drinks this water (the water in the well) will be thirsty again. But whoever drinks the water I give him will never thirst. Indeed, the water I give him will become in him a spring of water welling up to eternal life" (v. 13).

The Bible tells us her reaction in John 4:28: "Then, leaving her water jar, the woman went back to the town and said to the people.

'Come, see a man who told me everything I ever did. Could this be the Christ?' "

As a result of this encounter, during which she was filled with the "living water," her life would have a far-reaching impact. Indeed, "Many of the Samaritans from that town believed in him because of the woman's testimony." Talk about a jar of clay filled with a heavenly treasure. Talk about a woman who didn't let old labels control her future. Talk about a woman who refused to let what she used to be prevent her from becoming who she ought to be. Talk about a woman who had *been filled with the living water*.

Why did so many Samaritans turn to Jesus Christ? Why was the Samaritan woman at the well such a powerful vessel God could use? Because when people looked at her life, they couldn't dare say, "What a remarkable woman. I could never be like her." *No!* They were compelled to say, "What a *remarkable God* she has encountered. If there's a place for her in his kingdom, maybe there's a place for me. If he can use her, maybe he can use me, too!"

What exactly is meant by living water? Jesus clarifies the term a few chapters later:

> On the last and greatest day of the Feast, Jesus stood and said in a loud voice, "If a man is thirsty, let him come to me and drink. Whoever believes in me, as the Scripture has said, streams of living water will flow from within him." By this he meant the Spirit, whom those who believed in him were later to receive.
>
> John 7:37–39

Being filled with God, with the living water Jesus promised, is not a one-time event. It's a moment-by-moment way of life. Again, Andrew Murray says it well:

> All that the church and its members need for the manifestation of the mighty power of God in the world is the return to our true place, the place that belongs to us, both in creation and redemption, the place of absolute and unceasing dependence on God. . . .
>
> God, as creator, formed man to be a vessel in which He could show forth His power and goodness. Man was not to have in himself a fountain of life, or strength, or happiness. The ever-

living and only living One was intended each moment to be the communicator to man of all that he needed. Man's glory and blessedness was not to be independent, or dependent upon himself, but dependent on [God]. Man was to have the joy of receiving every moment out of the fullness of God.[1]

Christ is our very life; there is *no life* without water. We can only give that which we have received. After all, a vessel cannot *create* water. It can only pour forth that which is poured into it. In the same way, we must be filled with God's Spirit—filled with the Living Water—if we are to have anything to give others.

It seems to me that we face two dangers in the church today. And I think I've lived at both extremes. The first danger is this: water that remains in the vessel too long becomes stagnant. It's not enough to absorb sermon after sermon, Bible study after Bible study, Christian book upon Christian book, and never give back to others. If all we do is feed our own faith we'll become fat, lazy Christians. I've been there and I think many who fill the pews in our churches today are in precisely that predicament.

However, the second danger strikes me as even deadlier. And I've been guilty of this too: It's giving when you haven't been filled. It's speaking when you have no right to be heard. It's advising when no one asked for your counsel. It's speaking forth from the judgment and venom in your own heart, rather than the love and mercy that's in God's heart. It's a clay pot filled with nails and tacks, and coins and junk that dumps out on the kitchen floor. There's no beauty in it, only noise and a pervasive ugliness.

It's a self-appointed, amateur theologian telling a woman who is unable to conceive that God is punishing her. It's telling a man dying of cancer that there must be sin in his life. It's telling a paraplegic that he just doesn't have enough faith. It's poison from the pit of hell, not a message from the mouth of God. Take heed: before you attempt to pour anything into the precious life of another human being, *make sure you have first been filled.*

Throughout the rest of this week, we'll look at some specific things the Bible teaches we should be filled with and we'll discover

---

[1]Andrew Murray, *Believer's Secret of Waiting on God*, p.16.

some practical ways we can participate in the process of being filled.

1. Why was the Samaritan woman such an effective vessel God could use?

2. How had she previously tried to fill the "God-shaped void"? Do you think it worked? Why or why not?

3. What do you try to fill the "God-shaped void" with?

4. Can you think of an occasion when you "poured forth" words or deeds that weren't from God? What was the result?

5. Can you think of an occasion when you "poured forth" that which God had first poured into your life? What was the difference?

6. Which is a greater danger for you: absorbing without pouring forth, or pouring forth what you haven't first absorbed?

7. What key lesson did you glean from today's study?

To recap:

- A vessel cannot produce water. It can only pour forth that which has been poured into it.
- There are two dangers you must be alert to: Failing to give back the truths God pours into your life. And giving when you haven't been filled.

Day Two

Filled With Love and Joy

When we consider that which we must be filled with in order to be a vessel God can use, the fruit of righteousness—or fruit of the Spirit—should immediately spring to mind. For the next three days, let's explore exactly what these characteristics are. We'll look at each one in turn—starting today with love and joy—letting the Scriptures speak for themselves. As we do, prayerfully consider whether or not you are being filled to increasing measure with the fruit of the Holy Spirit. Galatians 5:22–25 tells us:

> But the fruit of the Spirit is love, joy, peace, patience, kindness, goodness, faithfulness, gentleness and self-control. Against such things there is no law. Those who belong to Christ Jesus have crucified the sinful nature with its passions and desires. Since we live by the Spirit, let us keep in step with the Spirit.

Love

When asked what the most important commandment was,

> Jesus replied: "Love the Lord your God with all your heart and with all your soul and with all your mind. This is the first and greatest commandment. And the second is like it: Love your neighbor as yourself." Matthew 22:37–39

The degree to which you demonstrate love to family and friends, neighbors, strangers, and even enemies, is an accurate measure of how filled you are with the Holy Spirit. What exactly does love entail? Is it an emotion that we must summon up? Once again, we turn to the Scripture:

> Love is patient, love is kind. It does not envy, it does not boast,

it is not proud. It is not rude, it is not self-seeking, it is not easily angered, it keeps no record of wrongs. Love does not delight in evil but rejoices with the truth. It always protects, always trusts, always hopes, always perseveres.

Love never fails. 1 Corinthians 13:4–8

If you want to get a good laugh, replace the word "love" with your own name and see how well it fits. Let me try: "Donna is patient" (That's the sound of my husband snickering in the background). Here's a good one: "Donna is not easily angered, she keeps no record of wrongs." (Excuse me, I need to get the sewing kit to put my husband back together. He has just fallen apart from laughter!)

Let's face it, if you had this love thing down, you wouldn't need to read a book about becoming a vessel God can use. The truth is, no one has ever *arrived* at perfect love on this side of eternity, except Jesus. Yet our goal is to become more and more like him each day:

You have heard that it was said, "Love your neighbor and hate your enemy." But I tell you: Love your enemies and pray for those who persecute you, that you may be sons of your Father in heaven. Matthew 5:43–45

Do you love your enemies or do you seek revenge? Do you harbor bitterness against those who have hurt you or are you quick to forgive? Jesus said we should evaluate our *love quotient* based on how we treat the people who treat us the *worst*. After all, "If you love those who love you, what reward will you get? Are not even the tax collectors doing that?" (Matthew 5:46). God does not get an ounce of glory when we love when loving is easy. That's something anyone can do. But only God can enable us to love those who have hurt us. And when we do, we get the world's attention. They see something *only God could do* and he gets the glory.

Several months ago, the news media were all running video footage of a bereaved mother screaming at her son's convicted murderer. She had a prepared statement, filled with venom, that she read in open court. No one could blame her, of course. This man had brutally cut short the life of her precious child. *Any normal person would feel that same rage.*

The event brought back to my mind another court scene. A

woman at our church in Philadelphia was widowed when her husband was brutally murdered. The culprit was caught and brought to trial. At the end of the case, she stood up and told the criminal that she forgave him and that she hoped he would one day come to know the God who meant so much to her husband. She then presented him with a Bible, with his name engraved on the front.

Which woman was a vessel God could use? One woman thought only of her grief and anger—and understandably so. Another woman thought only of God's Kingdom—and incomprehensibly so. As a result, I doubt anyone in that courtroom will ever be the same.

Joy

We tend to think of joy as something we experience, something that happens to us, but the Bible *commands us* to be joyful. And commands are not about feelings; they are about obedience. Joy is a choice; it's a decision we make about how we will respond to life's circumstances. So, joy is actually a very serious matter. In fact, we'll devote all of Week Ten to the subject of joy.

Any run-of-the-mill heathen can rejoice when the good times roll; what sets us apart—what enables God to bring glory to himself through our lives—is how we respond when the bad times roll. We rejoice, not only for our own sakes, but for the sake of a watching world. Remember, what is the sole reason for our existence? To *glorify God*. If we want to be a vessel God can use, then choosing to rejoice when everything around us says "mope and mumble" is an important first step.

1. Write out the 1 Corinthians 13 passage in the space provided below. Everywhere the word "love" occurs, substitute your own name.

2. How far are these descriptions from accurate? Do you have to roar with laughter? Note your reaction to this exercise:

3. Are you experiencing an increasing ability to demonstrate love to those who treat you badly? Think of a recent incident and describe how you handled it—for better or for worse!

4. Are you able to rejoice when times are hard? Or do you moan and groan? Again, try to think of a recent incident to support your response. Try to make an honest assessment of your current "fruit quotient."

5. What key lesson did you glean from today's study?

To recap:

- A vessel God can use must be filled with the fruit of the Holy Spirit.
- Two accurate measures of how filled we are: the love we show despite how we are treated, and the joy we demonstrate in spite of circumstances.

Day Three

Filled With Peace, Patience, Kindness, and Goodness

> Therefore, as God's chosen people, holy and dearly loved, clothe yourselves with compassion, kindness, humility, gentleness and patience. Bear with each other and forgive whatever grievances you may have against one another. Forgive as the Lord forgave you.
> Colossians 3:12–14

Filled With Peace

The Bible promises that we can experience a peace that defies logic. "And the peace of God, which transcends all understanding, will guard your hearts and your minds in Christ Jesus" (Philippians 4:7). Sounds good, but *how*? How can we be filled with peace that transcends all understanding? Fortunately, God doesn't leave us in the dark or say, "You guys figure it out for yourselves." It is to *God's glory* that we be filled, for it is then that we are a vessel through which he can accomplish his work. *He wants to fill us with peace even more than we want to be filled.*

The answer is found right in the next two verses: "Finally, brothers, whatever is true, whatever is noble, whatever is right, whatever is pure, whatever is lovely, whatever is admirable—if anything is excellent or praiseworthy—think about such things. Whatever you have learned or received or heard from me, or seen in me—put it into practice. And the God of peace will be with you" (Philippians 4:8–9).

Again, peace isn't something we passively wait for. Colossians 3:15 tells us to "Let the peace of Christ rule in your hearts." That's a command. Second Timothy 2:22–23 puts it even stronger: "Flee the evil desires of youth, and pursue righteousness, faith, love and *peace*[emphasis added], along with those who call on the Lord out of a pure heart. Don't have anything to do with foolish and stupid arguments, because you know they produce quarrels."

Peace is not only something we should strive to be filled with in the quiet moments when we're home alone; it's an attitude we need to overflow with when we interact with others. And, again, the Bible makes no bones about it. *This is hard work!* "Make every effort to live in peace with all men and to be holy; without holiness no one will see the Lord" (Hebrews 12:14).

If we had more peacemakers in the church, and fewer troublemakers, wouldn't that make an incredible difference? Wouldn't that bring glory to God and people into his Kingdom? You better believe it. How many people have walked away from the faith because of disillusionment over a church split? How many people never came to Christ because the church was too busy fighting and bickering to reach out? How many more are "turned off" to Christianity because of what they see going on in the church?

You know what the opposite of a peacemaker is? It's *someone who is full of herself.* People who want to pursue their agenda, their ideas, who think they alone have the corner on truth are the scourge of every church. I know, because I've been one myself. It goes back to our study on the importance of being *emptied of self.* Until we are emptied, we can't be a channel of peace. There's just too much emotional and spiritual garbage cluttering the way.

Certainly there are times in the church when we need to take a stand, such as when God's Word is being compromised. Or when a sister is living in sin, we must have the courage to confront in a loving way. Nevertheless, "If it is possible, as far as it depends on you, live at peace with everyone" (Romans 12:18). A woman who lives at peace with herself and others is a vessel God can use.

Filled With Patience

Today's verse from Colossians urges us, as God's chosen people, to "Bear with each other and forgive whatever grievances you may have against one another. Forgive as the Lord forgave you" (Colossians 3:13). You see, patience and forgiveness are vitally linked. I have an old poster that reads, "Please be patient; God isn't finished with me yet." We can endure each other's antics *as long as we don't hold a grudge*. If we hold on to every offense and refuse to forgive, we'll quickly run out of patience.

Our emotions are like a storehouse. We can only store up a certain amount of hard feelings before we burst forth in anger, bitterness, and resentment. That's why unforgiving people are also impatient people; their storehouse is always on the verge of overflowing. I used to be like that (still can be sometimes). My heart would be so full of bitterness, and my mind would be so occupied with years of recollections about who offended me and who took me for granted that the minute someone would "step on my toes," I would just explode. I was afraid that if I forgave the people who had hurt me that would be like saying what they did to me was okay. Then I learned that forgiving doesn't make them right; forgiving sets me free.

Are you an impatient person? Examine your heart and you will discover that your real problem may be an *unforgiving* heart. Clinging to old hurts will not benefit you in any way. It will, however, prevent you from becoming the useful, overflowing vessel God designed you to be. Proverbs 19:11 says, "A man's wisdom gives him patience; it is to his glory to overlook an offense." When we are patient with others, we can forgive, we can overlook offenses. And when we forgive, we'll find we have an entire storehouse *filled with patience*.

Kindness and Goodness

> For this very reason, *make every effort* to add to your faith goodness; and to goodness, knowledge; and to knowledge, self-control; and to self-control, perseverance; and to perseverance, godliness; and to godliness, brotherly kindness; and to brotherly kindness, love. For if you possess these qualities in increasing measure, they will keep you from being ineffective and unproductive in your knowledge of our Lord Jesus Christ.
>
> 2 Peter 1:5–8

Some people are just *nice*, don't ya think? God made 'em nice and that's the way they're gonna stay. He gave them the *niceness gene*, but do you ever suspect you must have been "hiding behind the door" when God handed out that gene? Well, it does seem that some people have an abundance of innate kindness and goodness, while the rest of us struggle along.

But what does the Bible say? It says *make every effort . . . to add to your faith goodness . . . and brotherly kindness.* Make every effort implies, again, that this is hard work. We don't passively wait to *be filled* with kindness and goodness. We actively seek to be filled. And why? "For if you possess these qualities in increasing measure, they will keep you from being ineffective and unproductive in your knowledge of our Lord Jesus Christ."

It is possible to have knowledge of our Lord Jesus Christ, and still be ineffective and unproductive. Isn't that a sobering thought? The Bible doesn't guarantee that all of us will be used to further his Kingdom. God can use women like us, but we will have to *make every effort* to add to our faith, kindness, and goodness.

While it's true that God often chooses the most unlikely vessels to work through, you can't stay where you are and go with God. Yes, God was willing to work through Rahab the Harlot, but she had to be willing to forsake her people and go with the Israelites. God was willing to work through the impetuous Peter, but he had to leave his fishing business and follow Christ. Abraham left Ur of the Chaldees. Moses had to leave Egypt, tend sheep for forty years, return to Egypt and leave again with God's people. David had to leave behind tending sheep to do battle with Goliath, and later to become King of Israel. It's a pattern throughout Scripture.

God accepts us where we are, but he wants us to continue on. Not only for the sake of his Kingdom, not only so that we can be vessels fit for his use, but for our own sake. Because he made us and he knows how we're wired. He knows that life will be better for us, if we *make every effort* to be *filled with kindness and goodness.* He knows that only then can we fulfill the very purpose for which we were created: to be a vessel reflecting the glory of God.

1. Are you a peacemaker or a troublemaker in the church? Examine your heart. Give evidence of your response.

2. What is the link between patience and forgiveness. Have you seen this link in your own life? How?

3. Who are you most impatient with? Is it possible that the real problem is an unforgiving attitude toward that person? What do you need to forgive?

4. How is it possible for someone who truly knows the Lord to live an unproductive and ineffective life? How can they fail to become a vessel God can use?

5. What key lesson did you glean from today's study?

To recap:

- God meets us where we are, but we can't stay where we are and go with God.
- It is possible to know the Lord Jesus Christ and still be ineffective and unproductive.
- The Bible urges us to *make every effort* to be filled with the fruit of the Spirit. Not only so we will be useful vessels through which God can work, but for our sake as well.

Day Four

Filled With Faithfulness, Gentleness, and Self-Control

Faithfulness

> Let love and faithfulness never leave you; bind them around your neck, write them on the tablet of your heart. Then you will win favor and a good name in the sight of God and man.
>
> Proverbs 3:3–4

According to *Strong's Exhaustive Concordance*, a faithful person is stable, trustworthy, established, certain, and true. To be faithful means you know exactly what you believe and you stand by it. We need to listen to the words of Elijah, who went before the people and said, "How long will you waver between two opinions? If the LORD is God, follow him" (1 Kings 18:21).

Do you waver between two opinions? Maybe in your mind you are convinced that your life must be filled with Christ; that your agenda must make way for his. How about the way you live your daily life? Do you always live as if you believe your highest calling is to present yourself as an empty vessel, waiting to be filled with the things of God? If you're like me, on many, many days, you are far too filled with yourself—your own plans and agenda—to have even the tiniest place for God. The truth is, God doesn't inhabit tiny places. He is either Lord *of all* or he is not Lord *at all*.

So, are you filled with faithfulness? Are you stable and trustworthy? Are you established in the faith—not only mentally but in your heart? Do you live your life with absolute certainty that God can accomplish through you all he has purposed? One of my favorite passages in the Bible is Elizabeth greeting Mary, who is pregnant with Jesus. She says, "Blessed is she who has believed that what the Lord has said to her will be accomplished!" (Luke 1:45). Isn't that a beautiful promise? Oh, how blessed our lives will be if we will only *believe that what the Lord has said to us will be accomplished.* If only we will be faithful to believe and follow.

Gentleness

Here's a passage I really don't like and we've managed to steer clear of it so far. Unfortunately, we can't avoid it any longer:

> Your beauty should not come from outward adornment, such as braided hair and the wearing of gold jewelry and fine clothes. Instead, it should be that of your inner self, the unfading beauty of a gentle and quiet spirit, which is of great worth in God's sight.   1 Peter 3:3–4

There are two things I don't like about this verse. First of all, I like to dress well and second, I *love* to talk, talk, talk! Is this verse saying I should look frumpy and never breathe a word? Many godly men and women throughout church history have believed so. Growing up, I lived within an hour of the Amish people of southeastern Pennsylvania. In case you're not familiar with them, they live and dress very simply. I mean *very* simply. They still drive horse-and-buggy, farm using horse and oxen, read by candlelight—in short, they forsake all modern conveniences. They dress in simple black clothing and the women keep their heads covered at all times. The women, it's safe to assume, remain very quiet.

Is this what this passage requires? Although I admire the Amish, I still love to wear purple and red and cream and whatever other color strikes my fancy. Yet I realize that real beauty doesn't rest in these things; it comes from within. The older I get, the happier I am to hear it.

So what *is* this inner beauty we are to be filled with? What is this gentle and quiet spirit the Bible commends? Let's look to Jesus, who said, "Take my yoke upon you and learn from me, for I am gentle and humble in heart, and you will find rest for your souls. For my yoke is easy and my burden is light" (Matthew 11:29–30).

We need to be gentle as Jesus was gentle. The only way we can be gentle in our dealings with others is if we enter into relationships with a humble heart. "Be completely humble and gentle; be patient, bearing with one another in love" (Ephesians 4:2). Here's how Andrew Murray explains it:

> Because Christ had thus humbled himself before God, and God was ever before him, he found it possible to humble himself before men, too. He was able to be the Servant of all. His humility was simply the surrender of himself to God, to allow the Father to do in him what he pleased, no matter what men around might say of him, or do to him.
>
> It is in this state of mind, in this spirit and disposition, that the redemption of Christ has its virtue and effectiveness. It is to bring us to this disposition that we are made partakers of Christ. This is the true self-denial to which our Savior calls us—the acknowledgment that self has nothing good in it except as an empty vessel which God must fill. And also that its claim to be or do anything may not for a moment be allowed. It is in this, above and before everything, in which the conformity to Jesus consists. It is the being and doing nothing by ourselves so that God may be all.
>
> Here we have the root and nature of true humility. We must learn of Jesus, how he is meek and lowly of heart. He teaches us where true humility takes its rise and finds its strength—in the knowledge that it is God who works all in all, that our place is to yield to him. . . .
>
> —from *Humility*

Gentleness is the outward expression of an inward reality: a heart that is humbled and a life that is emptied of self and yielded to God. So, "Let your gentleness be evident to all" (Philippians 4:5).

Self-Control

Now, here's a section of the book I should ask someone to "ghost write" for me! If there's one thing that's gotten me into more trouble in my life, it's a lack of self-control. I can't control my tongue, so I say stupid and tactless stuff that hurts others and gets me into hot water. I can't control my appetite, so I battle with that ever-creeping-upward scale in the bathroom. I can't control my activities, so I live at two extremes: doing nothing and doing too much. I often say I have two speeds: coma and frenzy. Neither is pleasing to God.

Come to think of it, maybe I do have a bit of wisdom to share about self-control. I've learned quite a bit about how *not* to be self-controlled. I know what doesn't work: trying to change from the outside. Like trying to force myself to keep quiet. Or trying to force myself to be the next Mrs. Clean by reading a book or attending a seminar. Trying to force myself to get thin and fit by signing up for a fad diet or the local aerobics class.

Outward attempts at self-control won't yield long-term results. You've got to change from the inside out. Don't look to yourself or to a program; look to God. Self-control is a fruit of the Holy Spirit. As you are increasingly filled with the Holy Spirit, you will be filled to increasing measure with self-control. I don't know about you, but I say, "Fill 'er up!"

1. Are you faithful or do you waver between two opinions? Maybe you are firm in your beliefs mentally, but how about the way you actually live?

2. Are you humble enough to be gentle with others?

3. Do you struggle with lack of self-control? In what areas? As you review problem areas, ask God for help. Remember, programs don't work; the Holy Spirit does.

4. Are you seeing the fruit of the Spirit manifested in your life in ever increasing measure? Don't give a quick reply. Sit before the Lord and meditate on each of the character qualities. Ask him to show you where you need to grow. Write what you hear:

5. What key lesson did you glean from today's study?

To recap:

- Be faithful to live as if you really believe the things you say you believe.
- Be humble enough to deal gently with others.
- Self-control doesn't come from a program; it comes from the Holy Spirit.

Day Five

Take Time to Refill the Vessel

Observe the Sabbath day by keeping it holy, as the LORD your
God has commanded you. Six days you shall labor and do your
work, but the seventh day is a Sabbath to the LORD your God.

Deuteronomy 5:12

Remember the old Jackson Browne tune "Running on Empty"?
Well, that's what far too many of us try to do. We run and run, we
do and do, until we can't do any more. Unfortunately, running on
empty is a formula for disaster. If there isn't any oil in your car, for
instance, it won't be long before you destroy your engine. Then, you
have two very expensive options: put in a new engine or buy a new
car.

The really depressing part of that scenario, of course, is realizing
that you could have easily prevented the disaster in the first place
with an oil change, check, or lube job. Unfortunately, you waited too
long, and now that same simple procedure that could have worked
wonders is completely useless.

Our spirit is like that in a sense. It's a vessel that needs to be
filled, oiled, maintained. If we fail to do routine spiritual mainte-
nance, if we neglect to refill our spiritual tanks, we're gonna give out.
It's just a matter of time. An empty vessel isn't going anywhere; it's
left by the side of the road, unfit for service. That's why I think setting
aside the Sabbath is so important.

The Sabbath is not just a day for lying around or catching up on
housework. It's a day to reflect on where we've been and where God
wants us to go in the future. In order to facilitate this process, I've
developed The Weekly Evaluation Worksheet. God *often speaks to me
most clearly on these quiet Sunday afternoons, when I'm willing to sit*

still and let my heart and mind reflect upon how I lived my life for the past week. Too often, we live our lives in a whirlwind. We have good intentions, but time zips by so rapidly we can barely catch our breath.

Ideally, you should find a quiet place and time. If weather permits and you have access to a park or picnic area, all the better. Take out your weekly calendar (if you have one) and reflect on the events and the people you encountered. Ask God to refresh your memory, to bring to mind moments when he was able to work through you or situations you should have handled differently.

On the following page is a sample Weekly Evaluation Worksheet. You may want to create your own list of reflective questions. The important thing is to use this time for refilling.

Some weeks, the answers will disappoint you. Reflection can be painful, yet it is so very necessary. Researchers surveyed a large group of people over age ninety and asked what they would do differently if they could live their lives over. One of the top three answers was "I would reflect more." Reflect and refill so you can remain *a vessel God can use*.

Once you've completed your weekly evaluation, re-write your priorities for the coming week onto a Post-It™ note and stick it where you'll see it often.

Throughout this week, we looked at the importance of being filled and constantly refilled with the living water of God's Spirit. We looked at the fruits of the Holy Spirit as an accurate way to evaluate how full (or empty) our vessels are. The more we are filled with the living water, the more fruit our lives will produce. Then, today we looked at the vital step of refilling the vessel by setting aside a Sabbath day of rest and reflection. If you want to be used by God, keep your vessel filled to overflowing.

Weekly Evaluation Worksheet

1. Am I listening for and hearing God's voice? What is he saying to me?

2. Am I increasingly manifesting the fruit of the Spirit: love, joy, peace, patience, kindness, goodness, faithfulness, gentleness, and self-control? What areas look encouraging? What needs prayer?

3. What did God teach me in my quiet times?

4. Which priorities did I live by?

5. Which priorities did I neglect?

6. What new thing did I learn—about life, God, my family, and the people around me?

7. What are my specific priorities (where is God directing me) for the coming week?

The Fourth Requirement for becoming a vessel God can use is:

Be *filled* and constantly refilled with the Living Water of the Holy Spirit.

1. What changes do you need to make in the way you honor the Sabbath?

2. How else is God challenging you to refill?

3. Complete the Weekly Evaluation for the past week. Note your reaction to the exercise:

4. What key lesson did you glean from today's study?

5. What was "This Week's Focus"?

6. What are the first four requirements for becoming a vessel God can use?

To recap:

- When we honor the Sabbath, we set aside time to reflect on where we've been and where God is directing us.
- Refilling is critical if we want to remain a vessel God can use.

Week Eight: Waiting

This Week's Focus:

Waiting to Hear God's Voice

This Week's Focus Verse:

I wait for the LORD, my soul waits, and in his word I put
my hope. My soul waits for the Lord more than watchmen
wait for the morning, more than watchmen
wait for the morning.

Psalm 130:5–6

Day One

God Speaks to His People

This week, we're going to take a break from the "Five Requirements" to focus our attention on an incredible privilege—the privilege of hearing God speak. In 1989, Lynne Rienstra (to whom this book is dedicated) sent me a Bible study guide called *Experiencing God*, by Henry Blackaby. She enclosed a note saying the study was among the most life-changing she'd ever encountered. Well, when Lynne puts her seal of approval on something, she gets my attention. I immediately undertook the study. Before I had completed the fourth week, I knew Lynne was right. So I called the publisher and ordered twenty copies, which I promptly gave to the people I cared about most.

As I write these words, I am again working through *Experiencing God* with a group of women in my church. It's my fourth time through, yet it is just as powerful. Well, the reason I'm telling you so much about *Experiencing God* is because I am so deeply indebted to Henry Blackaby for the material we will study this week. (Indeed, his influence has been so profound I'm sure it is felt throughout this book.)

And now that you have only three weeks remaining in this study, you are probably thinking about what to do next. Well, why not study *Experiencing God*? One word of warning: It is not enough to buy the *book*, which is available in bookstores. What you really want is the *workbook*, which can only be ordered through the Baptist Sunday School Board. If possible, ask your church to order the *Experiencing God* Video Cassettes as well. Call them at 1–800–458-BSSB and tell them I sent you. You can also write to:

Baptist Sunday School Board
127 Ninth Avenue North
Nashville, TN 37234

The fundamental premise that Blackaby sets forth—and which we will explore together this week—is this: God has always spoken to his people. God still speaks to his people. He speaks to you, but you may not be listening. Maybe you're just not sure how to listen or what you should be listening for. Maybe you've been too busy to *take time* to listen.

Do you consistently allow time to be still before God? Do you *ever* allow time to be still before God? Do you actively listen for his voice? If you haven't been listening, you should not be surprised if you are not hearing him. Maybe you feel that God is silent or at least he doesn't have anything to say to you. Rest assured, God wants to communicate with you. He longs for you to hear his voice and walk in close fellowship with him.

Whatever the case, *if you can't hear God speaking to you, you've got a fundamental problem at the very heart of your Christian life.* If you can't hear God speaking, the problem isn't with God, the problem is with you.

Now, I know that sounds harsh, but sometimes love must be tough. And now that we've spent seven weeks together, you know I'm the kind of friend who tells it like it is. I love you enough to tell you the truth! *Nothing in this ten-week study is more important than this issue right here.* So stop right now and write out a prayer of response to God. Either thank him for allowing you to hear him speaking or plead with him to open your heart that you might hear his voice. I promise you, he is so very willing! He is speaking, and he wants you to hear.

I believe writing out your prayers, or journaling, is one of the most effective ways that we can hear God speaking. As we put pen to paper, ideas spring from deep within our hearts. We open ourselves up in a way we're often afraid to when speaking. And writing forces us to stay focused, rather than allowing our minds to drift off. Try writing out your prayers for a week and see the difference it can make.

Let's look at the witness of Scripture, beginning with how God spoke in the Old Testament: "In the past God spoke to our forefathers through the prophets at many times and in various ways . . ." (Hebrews 1:1). Specifically, God spoke through:

- Angels (Genesis 16)
- Visions (Genesis 15)
- Dreams (Genesis 28:10–19)
- The burning bush (Exodus 3:2)
- The use of the Urim and Thummim (Exodus 28:30)
- Symbolic actions (Jeremiah 18:1–10)
- A gentle whisper (1 Kings 19:12)
- Miraculous signs (Exodus 8:20–25)

"How God spoke in the Old Testament is not the most important factor. *That* He spoke is the crucial point. Those He spoke to *knew* it was God, and they *knew* what He was saying."[1] In the gospels, God spoke directly through Jesus. When Jesus left the earth, he sent the Holy Spirit. Beginning with Pentecost and until the present day, God speaks to us through his Holy Spirit. "But when he, the Spirit of truth, comes, he will guide you into all truth. He will not speak on his own; he will speak only what he hears, and he will tell you what is yet to come" (John 16:13).

We tend to think God is in the business of keeping secrets, as if he is sitting on his heavenly throne with his arms crossed, saying, "You guys figure it out for yourselves." Nothing could be further from the truth. Have you stopped to consider how many miracles God performed to prepare and preserve his Word for us? Would an absentee God go to all that trouble?

Would you, a mere human, treat *your children* like that? What kind of parent would bring a child into this world *and then never speak to him, never give him any instructions, any comfort, any love?* What kind of a parent would not want to cultivate a deep love relationship

---

[1]Blackaby, p. 73.

with her child? And isn't it obvious that such a relationship would require constant and clear communication? How much more does our heavenly Father desire to communicate with his children?

Can you imagine how much trouble your kids would get into if you *never* gave them any instructions? Their lives would be a total disaster. The same is true of us as God's children. If we're not getting our instructions from God, we should *expect* our lives to be a mess! Unfortunately, most of us don't even consider the possibility of listening for God's voice. We just go our merry way and occasionally toss up a "Dear God, Bless this mess" prayer.

Please take it from one of the world's foremost experts on making a mess of things (that's me): God has a better way. God will give you specific instructions for your life, if you will only listen and obey. What if you haven't received specific instructions from God on a particular matter? Should you just go ahead and do your own thing? No. "If you do not have clear instructions from God in a matter, pray and wait. Learn patience. Depend on God's timing. His timing is always right and best. Don't get in a hurry. He may be withholding directions to cause you to seek Him more intently. Don't try to skip over the relationship to get on with *doing*. God is more interested in a love relationship with you than He is in what you can do for Him."[2]

God still speaks. He loves you and wants to communicate with you. So listen!

1. How do you know that God speaks to his people?

2. List some of the ways God has spoken to his people throughout history.

---

[2]Ibid., p. 75.

3. What is more important: the method God used to speak or the fact that he did, indeed, speak? Why?

4. Think of an occasion when you received specific instructions from God concerning a matter. What was the result?

5. Now think of an occasion when you failed to consult God before making an important decision or taking a crucial step. What was the result?

6. Set aside 30 minutes to be still and listen for God's voice. You might meditate on Scripture, take a walk in a peaceful setting, or simply enter your prayer closet. Record what you believe God was saying to you. (Don't panic yet if you "didn't hear anything." We've got four more lessons to go, and you've got eternity to listen to God's voice.)

7. What key lesson did you glean from today's study?

To recap:

- God has always spoken to his people. He still does.
- God will give you specific instructions for your life, but you must wait on his timing.
- God continually seeks a love relationship with you.
- If you can't hear God speaking, you are in trouble at the heart of your Christian life.

Day Two

God Speaks Through a Donkey

There is no limit to the means God can use to speak to his people. If we won't listen to him through prayer or meditation on his Word, he'll just come up with more creative means. Like the time he spoke *through a donkey*:

Balaam got up in the morning, saddled his donkey and went with the princes of Moab. But God was very angry when he went, and the angel of the LORD stood in the road to oppose him. Balaam was riding on his donkey, and his two servants were with him. When the donkey saw the angel of the LORD standing in the road with a drawn sword in his hand, she turned off the road into a field. Balaam beat her to get her back on the road.

Then the angel of the LORD stood in a narrow path between two vineyards, with walls on both sides. When the donkey saw the angel of the LORD, she pressed close to the wall, crushing Balaam's foot against it. So he beat her again.

Then the angel of the LORD moved on ahead and stood in a narrow place where there was no room to turn, either to the right or to the left. When the donkey saw the angel of the LORD, she lay down under Balaam, and he was angry and beat her with his staff. Then the LORD opened the donkey's mouth, and she said to Balaam, "What have I done to you to make you beat me these three times?"

Balaam answered the donkey, "You have made a fool of me! If I had a sword in my hand, I would kill you right now."

The donkey said to Balaam, "Am I not your own donkey, which you have always ridden, to this day? Have I been in the habit of doing this to you?"

"No," he said.

Then the LORD opened Balaam's eyes, and he saw the angel of the LORD standing in the road with his sword drawn. So he bowed low and fell facedown.

The angel of the LORD asked him, "Why have you beaten your donkey these three times? I have come here to oppose you because your path is a reckless one before me. The donkey saw me and turned away from me these three times. If she had not turned away, I would certainly have killed you by now, but I would have spared her." Numbers 22:21–34

There are a number of incredible things about this story. The obvious, of course, is the talking donkey. Whenever I have a speaking engagement, I always re-read this passage. It reminds me that just because God may speak through me doesn't mean I'm some big-shot spiritual giant. He talked through a donkey. And most days, I've got a lot more in common with that donkey than I do with any spiritual giants. And if you're still not convinced that you don't have to be the perfect person to be a vessel God can use, what more proof do you need? Gee, not only don't you have to be a *perfect* person, you don't even have to be a *person*.

What really fascinates me about this story is Balaam's reaction. The guy doesn't even miss a beat. He jumps right into conversation with his donkey without stopping to think, "Hey, this is weird. What's going on here?" We're the same way. God sends the most unusual circumstances our way, trying to get our attention, but we just keep strolling casually along. The New Testament provides some additional insight into what motivated Balaam:

They have left the straight way and wandered off to follow the way of Balaam son of Beor, who loved the wages of wickedness. But he was rebuked for his wrongdoing by a donkey—a beast without speech—who spoke with a man's voice and restrained the prophet's madness. 2 Peter 2:15–16

Isn't it amazing how the pursuit of material possessions can make us turn a deaf ear to God? Everything around us may be crying out "stop," but we refuse to listen. Like the workaholic woman whose marriage is in absolute ruins; her children are on drugs and uncontrollable; the house has been seriously neglected; she has no friends and no life outside of her workplace; the stress has built up to the bursting point; her doctor warns her that a breakdown is imminent.

Yet, she never stops to say, "Hey, wait a minute. I must be on the wrong path. Maybe God is trying to tell me something."

When we come face-to-face with obstacles, we usually react exactly like Balaam. We strike out at whoever or whatever is closest to us. We've got an agenda to pursue and we resent anything that stands in our way.

Here's an irony worth pondering: We pray for God to *remove the obstacle*, when it may very well be that *God is the one who put the obstacle there*. The next time you're tempted to pray for God to change your circumstances, stop and think. Maybe God doesn't want to change the circumstances, *he wants to change you.*

When life goes awry, that's your clue that God is trying to speak to you. Pay attention! Pray. Study God's Word. Seek counsel from mature Christians. It goes without saying that we don't rely *solely* on circumstances for guidance. But when we evaluate circumstances in light of what the Holy Spirit is telling us through his Word, through prayer and through fellow believers (we'll look at these three in turn over the next three days), we can get a very clear indication of what God is saying.

Are there any donkeys talking to you? Listen up!

1. When Balaam's donkey began speaking to him, how did Balaam react?

2. Why was his reaction unusual? What does it tell us about where his heart was? What does it tell us about how willing he was to listen to God?

3. What are two things that can make us turn a deaf ear to what God is trying to say through our circumstances? Can you think of other things, as well?

4. What is the most unusual circumstance you have ever faced in your life? What did God teach you through that experience?

5. What is the most unusual way God has communicated with you?

6. Are there any "talking donkeys" in your path? Are you facing any difficult or unusual circumstances right now? What might God be trying to tell you?

7. What key lesson did you glean from today's study?

To recap:

- God can use a talking donkey—or anything else he chooses—to communicate with you.
- Pay attention to your circumstances. God may well be trying to speak to you through them.

Day Three

God Speaks Through His Word

All Scripture is God-breathed and is useful for teaching, rebuking, correcting and training in righteousness, so that the man of God may be thoroughly equipped for every good work.
                                                              2 Timothy 3:16–17

In Week 3, we looked at the importance of knowing God by knowing his Word. We come back to that topic today for a slightly different reason. Not only can we know who God is by studying his Word, not only can we know what he has done in the past, but we can gain insight into *what he wants to do now and in the future*. That's because the Bible is not just an historical document, not just an inspirational document, not just the source of good doctrine. Although it is all of those things and more, it is *also God's means of communicating with us* today. God speaks through his Word.

As you may have noticed, the Bible is a pretty thick book. You can't exactly read the entire thing every time you need guidance from God. Well, I guess you could. . . . Some people look for guidance from God's Word by flipping it open and dropping their finger randomly on the page. You can get in trouble like this, of course. Like the old story about the man who was having marriage trouble. He opened his Bible, and put his finger on the verse that said, "Judas went and hung himself." He didn't think that sounded right, so he flipped again and this time landed on, "What you must do, do quickly." Well, that's a pretty sad joke, I know. But what is *really sad* is God's people approaching God's Word in such a superstitious and haphazard manner.

There is a better way to find specific help from God's Word when you need it, right "while you're in the thick of it." Helen

Sturm, of Gilbert, Arizona, developed a Bible color-coding system that I think really makes it easier to hear God's voice through God's Word.

Let me give you an example. Whenever you find a passage that encourages you, use a pencil to color it blue. The next time you or someone you love is feeling blue, turn to your Bible and look for passages you've colored. (I just love marking my Bible and making it mine. However, if you don't wish to mark yours, you can write the passages on index cards using the right color magic markers.)

The rest of the coloring system is as follows. I've included the cues that help me remember which-color-for-which, but don't rely on your memory. Write out the coding system on an index card and tuck it in your Bible.

- Blue—Comfort, Encouragement (Blue is soothing; comfort when you're feeling blue.)
- Red—Holy Spirit (red flames, tongues of fire)
- Yellow—Promises (Sun brings promise of a new day.)
- Green—God's Greatness and God's Word
- Gray—Satan, Sin (Satan deceives us by leading us into gray areas.)
- Orange—Commands for Christian Living (When we obey his commands, our lives will shine like the noonday sun.)

For the next twenty minutes (at *least*), search through your Bible and color some of your favorite passages—passages that really speak to you. Also, look back at the Bible verses we've studied throughout the past eight weeks. Perhaps God spoke to you in a special way through some of those. If so, color them as well. Don't look at this as a coloring exercise; look at it as an opportunity to listen for God's voice.

1. What is one significant tool God uses to communicate with us?

2. What strategy can you use to make it easier for God to speak to you through his Word when facing a specific trial?

3. What key lesson did you glean from today's study?

To recap:

- God speaks through his Word.
- If you want to hear from God, read his Word and listen to what it says.
- Color-coding your Bible can help!

Day Four

God Speaks Through Us, Through His Word

G od not only speaks to us through his Word, he can also speak through us, through his Word. How? By turning Scripture into prayer. Every crisis known to humankind boils down to two simple questions: Is God in control? Does God love me? If God is in control and he loves us, then there are no crises, only circumstances sent by a loving God to bring us closer to himself. By praying Scripture, we can communicate that in a loving way to the people around us. We can be a vessel through which God can speak very directly.

How often are you "at a loss for words"? Well, you won't be if you know Scripture. How often have you said the *wrong* thing? Well, you won't if you know—and pray—Scripture. How do you know God's will for your life and help others find it for themselves? That's a question posed by many Christians every day of the week. While it's true that some things will remain a mystery, God speaks plainly about his will through his Word. Here again, highlighting portions of Scripture can help when you—or someone else—need specific direction.

When you not only base your prayer requests on Scripture, but actually turn Scripture into a prayer, you don't have to worry whether or not you are praying according to God's will—you are. Helen Sturm, who developed the Bible color-coding system we introduced yesterday, uses those highlighted portions to "pray Scripture." Try it. It will be a wonderful blessing for you and those whose lives you touch.

Choose a passage such as Psalm 1:3 and simply substitute the person's name. In this example, I will use my husband, Cameron.

> Cameron, I pray that you will be like a tree planted by streams of water, which yields its fruit in season and whose leaf does not wither. May whatever you do prosper.

Or I might pray Hebrews 13:30 for my daughter, Leah:

179

Leah, may the God of peace . . . that great Shepherd of the sheep, equip you with everything good for doing his will. Leah, I pray he may work in you what is pleasing to him, through Jesus Christ, to whom be glory for ever and ever. Amen.

My favorite blue verse is Lamentations 3:22–25. Here's how I turn it into a prayer:

I rest in you Lord, because your compassions never fail.
They are new every morning;
great is your faithfulness.
I say to myself, "The Lord is my portion;
therefore I will wait for him.
The Lord is good to me because my hope is in him,
to me because I seek him.

When your family faces impossible situations, you need to remember "all things are possible with God." He is King of Kings and Lord of Lords. So whenever you find a verse describing the power of God or the power of his Word, color it purple for royalty. A wonderful purple verse is Isaiah 46:9–10. As a family, you can pray:

Lord, we remember the former things, those of long ago;
We praise you that you are God, and there is no other.
You are God, and there is none like you.
Father, we thank you that you made known the end from the
beginning, from ancient times, what is still to come.
We know that your purpose will stand,
and you will do all that you please.

As a family, we rest in that.

I hope you enjoyed yesterday's exercise, looking up and coloring scriptures that spoke to you. We're going to do more of the same today. Look up the following passages which *speak to specific situations.* Color them for future reference. I've suggested the colors I would choose. However, you can use your own categories.

Prayers for Families
    Psalm 90:17 (Yellow)
    Ephesians 6:10–19 (Orange)

Prayers for Marriage
  Romans 15:5–7 (Yellow)
  Jeremiah 32:39–41 (Yellow)
Prayers for Husbands
  Jeremiah 17:7–8 (Orange)
  Ephesians 1:16–19 (Orange) and 3:14–19 (Blue)
  Colossians 1:9–13 (Orange)
Prayers for Children
  Psalm 32:8 (Yellow)
  Proverbs 4:10–13 (Orange)
  Colossians 1:9–13 (Orange)
Prayers of Encouragement
  Philippians 4:4–7 (Orange)
  Habakkuk 3:18–19 (Orange)
  Psalm 34: 1–10 (Orange) and 103: 8–13 (Blue)
  Isaiah 41:10 (Yellow)
  1 Thessalonians 3:11–13 (Orange)
  2 Thessalonians 3:5 (Blue)

And finally, my sisters, here is my prayer for *you* (color it blue): "May the Lord bless you, dear reader, as you pray in the Spirit on all occasions with all kinds of prayers and requests" (Ephesians 6:18).

1. How can we be sure that when we pray, we are praying according to God's will?

2. In what way did God speak to you through today's passages? Write out a prayer expressing the truths he laid on your heart.

3. What key lesson did you glean from today's study?

To recap:

- God speaks through us, especially when we speak his Word.
- When we turn God's Word into prayer, we know we are praying according to God's will.

Day Five

God Speaks to Us When We Pray

Do not be anxious about anything, but in everything, by prayer and petition, with thanksgiving, present your requests to God. And the peace of God, which transcends all understanding, will guard your hearts and your minds in Christ Jesus.

Philippians 4:6–7

When I became a Christian, one of my earliest lessons was about ACTS. (Thanks to Rob Rienstra, the vessel God used to teach me.) It's not about the Book of Acts, but the acronym ACTS, which stands for an approach to prayer. Using this simple strategy brings balance to your prayer life and helps you get beyond a gimme-gimme attitude to really hear what God is saying:

Adoration
Confession
Thanksgiving
Supplication

Adoration means worshiping God for his attributes. When we adore God, we honor him for who he is, not for what he does on our behalf. Reading the Psalms is a wonderful exercise in adoration. Also, revisit the material studied during Week 2, because the more you know about the character of our God, the easier it will be to adore him. And, the more clearly you will be able to identify his voice when he speaks, for God will never tell us to do anything contrary to his character.

Confession clears your mind and heart, knowing "When we confess our sins, he is faithful and just and will forgive us our sins and purify us from all unrighteousness" (1 John 1:9). It also reminds us that we have no right to make demands of a holy God, but should come before him in humility, ready to hear what he has to say.

Thanksgiving gives us the right perspective: God has already given us everything we need. In response to his goodness, we need to listen and discover how he wants to use us today to be a channel of his mercy and grace. (See Week 7, Day 5, "Filled With Gratitude" for specific suggestions on cultivating a thankful heart.)

Supplication is your opportunity to bring your requests before God. And now that you've adored him, confessed your sins, and called to mind all that you have to be thankful for, you're ready to intercede. Pray for your husband, your children, your neighbors, your pastor, and your church. Select a country in the news, and begin praying for its people.

> Christ meant prayer to be the great power by which his Church should do its work. . . . Our King upon the throne finds his highest glory in intercession; we shall find our highest glory in it too. Through it he continues his saving work, and can do nothing without it; through it alone we can do our work, and nothing avails without it. . . . The power of the Church to bless rests on intercession—*asking and receiving heavenly gifts to carry to men*. When, due to lack of teaching or spiritual insight, we trust in our own diligence and effort to include the world and the flesh, and work more than we pray, the presence and power of God are not seen in our work as we would wish. . . .
>
> Prayer links the King on the throne with the Church at his footstool. The Church, the human link, receives its divine strength from the power of the Holy Spirit who comes in answer to prayer.
>
> Prayer is still the appointed means for drawing down these heavenly blessings in power on ourselves and those around us. . . . We have now seen what power prayer has. It is the one power on earth that commands the power of heaven.[3]

So many wonderful things happen when we pray. The forces of darkness are driven back and the angelic hosts spring into action. I love the picture Frank Peretti paints in *Piercing the Darkness* (Crossway Books): our prayers are the fuel for angels' wings.

---

[3]Andrew Murray, *The Ministry of Intercessory Prayer*. (Bethany House Publishers), pp. 12–29.

The Holy Spirit often nudges us into action while we pray. We pray for a sick neighbor, and a still, small voice prompts us to bake a casserole. We pray for our pastor, and God prompts us to write a note of encouragement. Keep a notebook handy, so you can write down what you hear God telling you during your prayer time. Don't become distracted by details like when or how to follow-up. You can deal with that later, once you've finished praying.

This week we focused on the importance of waiting to hear God's voice. We received assurance that God speaks to his people—he always has and he always will. God speaks to us in a variety of ways, including circumstances. He often speaks through his Word and he also speaks *through us* through his Word. Most frequently, however, God speaks to us when we pray—especially when our prayer is grounded in a clear understanding of his Word, his will, and his ways.

Are you spending enough time in prayer to really hear all that God wants to say to you? God is always speaking. The question is, are we listening! Isn't it worth any sacrifice we might have to make in order to hear God? Pray about it and see what God says to you about your prayer life.

1. How much time do you now spend in prayer each day?

2. How much time would you like to spend?

3. Do you think you would hear God's voice more clearly if you set aside that amount each day? Why or why not?

4. What sacrifices or schedule adjustments are you willing to make to set aside time to listen for God's voice?

5. Look up the following verses and record any insights you glean on prayer.

Jeremiah 33:3

Matthew 21:22

John 14:13 and 15:17

Ephesians 6:18

Colossians 1:3 and 4:2

1 Thessalonians 5:17

1 Timothy 2:8

6. What key lesson did you glean from today's study?

7. What was "This Week's Focus"?

To recap:

- God speaks to us when we go to him in prayer.
- When we pray, the Holy Spirit will often speak to us about actions we need to take during our time with him *and* after we finish praying.

Week Nine: Pouring

This Week's Focus:

Pouring Out Your Life In Ministry As God Directs

This Week's Focus Verse:

Teach us to number our days aright,
that we may gain a heart of wisdom.

Psalm 90:12

Day One

Go With God

The fifth and final Requirement for becoming a vessel God can use is: "Pouring out your life in ministry as God directs." Notice that it is not enough to pour your life where *you* think you are needed; it's not enough to "attempt great things for God" or simply to "find a need and fill it." Your life will be as effective as you are responsive to God's direction. That's why we spent last week on the importance of waiting to hear God's voice before taking action.

God is not trying to keep secrets from us. He wants each of us to become a vessel he can use in this world. Unfortunately, so many of our ministry efforts leave us feeling bitter and exhausted, rather than joyous and energized. Why is that? It's because we're trying to do things for God rather than letting him accomplish his purposes through us.

> As truly as God by His power once created, so truly by that same power must God, every moment, maintain. Man need only look back to the origin of existence and he will acknowledge that he owes everything to God. Man's chief care, his highest virtue, and his only happiness, now and through all eternity, is to present himself as an empty vessel in which God can dwell and manifest His power and goodness.
>
> —*Humility*, Andrew Murray

When we're trying to do "great things for God," what we're really doing is pursuing our own agenda and our own vision of what should be done, all the while forgetting that God has an eternal agenda. In short, we leave God behind rather than going with God.

As Henry Blackaby says in *Experiencing God*, "We must remain in the master's hand and be moldable. Understanding what God is about to do where I am is more important than telling God what I want to do for him." While we're off baking casseroles for the sick, God is waiting patiently to use us in his work. Nothing wrong with casseroles for the sick, mind you. But are you making casseroles because that's where God directed you? Or are you making casseroles to impress God or to win approval or to make yourself feel better or because so-and-so will make you feel guilty?

It's possible to do all the right things with all the wrong motives:

We can witness . . . out of pride.

We can serve others . . . so they will admire us.

We can go to church . . . out of habit.

We can pray . . . to get what we want.

As long as we're operating on wrong motives or just flying on autopilot, we're leaving God behind. We're not going with God, we're going on our own. And that's not how he wants us to go.

When you think about it, there's so much that needs to be done in this world. It's tempting to just jump in wherever we see a need. In fact, it's often said, "Find a need and fill it." While there's some truth in that, let's first be sure it's a need God wants filled. Maybe God wants that need *left unmet*, so that person will see his need for salvation, repentance, or a dozen other good reasons why God allows us to endure hard times. Did you ever think of that? When you go in to fix and meddle and rescue, not only are you not helping, you may well be doing harm.

So, if it's wrong to try to fill every need we see, how should we discern where God wants us to go? As Charles Hummel points out in his booklet, *The Tyranny of the Urgent* (InterVarsity Press): "Jesus did not respond to every request. He channeled most of his time and energy into twelve men. Yet he was able to say, 'I have brought you glory on earth by completing the work *you* gave me to do' " [emphasis added]. Notice the difference between the work *other people* wanted Jesus to do and the work *his Father* gave him to do. Plenty of blind men remained blind. Plenty of sick people stayed sick. Many people died but were not raised from the dead, as Lazarus was. How did Jesus know when to intervene and when not to? How did he know which needs to fill and which his father wanted to remain unfilled? He was able to do so because he was always abiding in the Father's presence. "He discerned the Father's will day by day in a life of prayer. By this means He warded off the urgent and accomplished the important."[1]

We should do likewise. Again, the key is: Go with God. Don't assume you know what needs to be done just because you see a situation and have a possible solution. That's arrogance! That's pride and God says he hates it! Isn't it amazing? What we consider "being nice" God can actually despise? His ways are definitely not our ways. That's why it's so important to go with God, if we want to be a vessel he can use.

1. Have you ever jumped in to meet a need and later realized God didn't want that need met? Describe.

2. How is the Father calling you to abide in him; to discern his will as Jesus did?

3. What key lesson did you glean from today's study?

To recap:

- Go with God.
- God is not trying to keep secrets from you. He wants to direct you into his will, to accomplish his work.
- Don't just "find a need and fill it." It may be that God wants that need left unmet.
- We can do all the right things for all the wrong reasons. We should only do that which God directs us to do, as an act of obedience.

---

[1]from *Tyranny of the Urgent.*

Day Two

Big-Picture Direction

There are different kinds of gifts, but the same Spirit. There are different kinds of service, but the same Lord. There are different kinds of working, but the same God works all of them in all men.   1 Corinthians 12:4–6

As we have already seen, God will direct you day-by-day. Nevertheless, he has also equipped you with specific interests and abilities and laid on your heart specific concerns. By making a careful study of the type of vessel he made you to be, you gain a good understanding of how he probably intends to use you. You can grasp the "big-picture" of where God wants to direct you throughout your life. Who you are *is an important part of God's direction—it is key to understanding how he wants to use you.*

Zig Ziglar, internationally known author and speaker, poses the question, "Are you a wandering generality or a meaningful specific?" As we've already learned, God can and will use whomever he chooses. But a "meaningful specific" is often far more usable than one who lacks direction. This issue came up recently in our women's Bible study as we were discussing "hearing God's voice" in *Experiencing God.* The author, Henry Blackaby, emphasizes the importance of staying alert to where God is at work and then joining him in that work. As one woman pointed out, however, you could have a nervous breakdown in a week if you joined in on everything God is doing in the world around you.

When you see God at work, how do you know whether or not he wants to use you in a particular situation? Finding a need, then trying to fill it, is *not* a valid approach. One key, I believe, is cultivating a clear life mission. That is, discerning what the Father wants you to accomplish *in your lifetime*. Do you know what your life mission is? Do you have a clear sense of what God uniquely created you to do? Are you a meaningful specific? Or are you a wandering generality?

Often, the busiest woman around is a wandering generality. She's doing a little of this and a little of that, and not really getting anywhere at all. She may even carry out her varied tasks very efficiently. However, she'll never make a lasting mark on her world until she discovers God's mission for her. It's painfully easy to spot a woman who lacks a sense of mission. She's running as fast as she can, but it's never fast enough. She allows everyone else to set her priorities. Her husband wants her to take up bowling. Her children want her to chauffeur them from cheerleading, to gymnastics, to the mall, to Susie's house. (And that's just Monday.) The missions committee wants her to plan the fall conference. A friend wants her to join aerobics. Another friend recruited her for the choir. And on and on and on.

These activities are all wonderful, provided you do them in response to God's calling upon your life. However, if your primary motivation is winning the approval of others, trouble waits ahead. If you hunger for man's approval, you'll find it almost impossible to say no to any request for your time. Unfortunately, very often when you're saying yes to people, you're saying no to God.

We've said it before, but we can't emphasize it enough. God doesn't want us to *do* anything for him. He doesn't need our help or suggestions. He wants us to be available *so he can do his work through us*. Often when we're busy "doing things for God," we are missing out on our real mission.

Frequently when women express a desire to manage their time more effectively, they mean, "How can I juggle all the 'stuff' I've jammed into my life more efficiently?" Or they mean, "I can't get motivated to do anything; how can I become more self-disciplined?" The answer to both questions is "Discover your life mission and the rest (well, most of it) will take care of itself." When you step into God's plan, when you are simply a vessel through which he can accomplish his work, he provides the energy and the means. It's nothing short of miraculous. You'll see!

For example, I wrote my first book, *Homemade Business*, in just three months, during which my infant daughter cried day and night with colic. I stood at the keyboard with her in a Snugli™ pouch, bouncing up and down. If I stopped bouncing, she would start screaming. On a good day, I got five hours sleep. Only God knows how we did it. It's just a blur in my mind.

Yet God worked through me to bring a timely message to more than 70,000 women. *God can do his work through you, even when you don't understand how.* As we surely know by now, he delights in choosing the most unlikely vessels. So, how can you discover your life mission? How can you obtain "big-picture" direction concerning where God wants you to flow? It takes reflection, prayer, and honest feedback from others. God is *not trying to keep secrets from you.* Ask him to give you "big-picture direction" for your future, and to guide you in making daily choices. The one who called you is faithful, and he will do it.

> "For I know the plans I have for you," declares the LORD, "plans to prosper you and not to harm you, plans to give you hope and a future. Then you will call upon me and come and pray to me, and I will listen to you. You will seek me and find me when you seek me with all your heart." Jeremiah 29:11–13

If you are one of those women who allows herself to be pulled in a million different directions, here's a simple little exercise that may help you distinguish between what God wants you to do and what everyone else wants you to do:

1. If you were to die tomorrow, what do you want people to remember? Write whatever comes to mind.

2. What do you feel passionately about? If the subject comes up you perk up and can't stop talking.

3. When you go to a bookstore or library, what section do you drift toward?

4. What do people compliment you about? What activities do you excel in?

5. What did you dream of doing when you were ten years old? Think back. You may just discover that that little girl knew a lot more about who God created you to be than you realize.

6. If you could only do one activity, all day, every day, for the rest of your life, what would it be?

7. Has God laid a special burden on your heart—for a group of people, a country, a ministry? Maybe you made a special vow to him at a youth camp long ago. It's likely that God has tried, many times in many ways, to communicate your life mission. Reflect.

8. Now, summarize your thoughts in a few sentences. That may be the blueprint for defining your life mission. Seek God's guidance in fine-tuning it. Write it in the front of your Bible (or on an index card, tucked in your Bible) and purposefully review it daily for the rest of your life.

9. What key lesson did you glean from today's study?

To recap:

- When we have the "big-picture" it's easier to discern God's direction in the "little" things.
- Understanding who God created you to be is a vital part of becoming a vessel God can use.

Day Three

Be Willing to Act

On Day Two, we looked at the danger of jumping in where God has not directed us. Today, we'll look at an even greater danger: failing to take action when God *has* directed us. When God speaks to us about a specific need (as he often does when we pray—see Week Eight, Day Five), that's our cue to take action. It does no good to call a friend a month after the Holy Spirit's prompting. *She needed you then.* For all you know, that friend may have been contemplating suicide or facing some other life-changing crisis. *Take action when God directs.*

Throughout this book, we've focused on the inward reality, the inward qualities of a vessel God can use. There's a time to cultivate the inner life, and it's an area we too often neglect. But there's also a time to take action. There's also a time when we put our faith where our hands and feet are. The book of James is my favorite and it has much to say about putting faith into action:

> What good is it, my brothers, if a man claims to have faith but has no deeds? Can such faith save him? Suppose a brother or sister is without clothes and daily food. If one of you says to him, "Go, I wish you well; keep warm and well fed," but does nothing about his physical needs, what good is it? In the same way, faith by itself, if it is not accompanied by action, is dead.
> But someone will say, "You have faith; I have deeds."
> Show me your faith without deeds, and I will show you my faith by what I do. James 2:14–18

What good is a faith that never touches another human life? What good is a vessel that sits on the shelf looking pretty? None whatsoever. When God shows you what he wants you to do, get involved immediately. Listen carefully, though. Sometimes God will give you a preview of things to come and what he wants you to do now is "prepare, adjust, and train." You may have to wait days, weeks, even years, for the instruction to "Go." One thing you can be sure of, though. When God gives you the signal to "Go" he also will give you the wisdom and the strength to accomplish his purposes in his timing. You'll get more done in one month of flowing where God directs than you will in a lifetime of doing your own thing for God.

Again: *You will accomplish more in one month of flowing where God directs than you will in a lifetime of doing your own thing for God.* Search your heart to see if you really believe that. Then examine your life to see if you actually *live* like you believe that. Indicate below what specific evidence you have uncovered that indicates whether you are flowing with God or doing your own thing.

I must add one caveat, however. Just because you are flowing where God directs, doesn't mean everything will *flow smoothly.* No way! We live in a fallen world, so you'll face opposition from people who disapprove of your methods, question your motives, or simply misunderstand you. Who knows, you might even deserve some of the criticism. You are, after all, only human. We also have an enemy, prowling around like a roaring lion, looking for someone to devour (1 Peter 5:8).

Nevertheless, it's better to be in the arena of God's direction than sitting on the shelf. The following poem illustrates what it means, in a very practical, action-oriented way, to be a vessel God can use:

"I Will Do More"

I will do more than belong, I will participate.
I will do more than care, I will help.
I will do more than believe, I will practice.
I will do more than be fair, I will be kind.
I will do more than forgive, I will love.
I will do more than earn, I will enrich.
I will do more than teach, I will serve.

197

I will do more than live, I will grow.
I will do more than be friendly, I will be a friend.
Think and pray on this . . . and then act.[2]

1. Note your response to the poem "I Will Do More." Give a specific example for each, of how you can

Participate

Help

Practice

Be Kind

Love

Enrich

[2]From St. Paul's Evangelical Lutheran Church, Sassamansville, Penna.

Serve

Grow

Be a Friend

Act

2. Can you think of a situation where God directed you to get involved, but you refused to take action? What was the result?

3. Is there something, right now, that God is asking you to do? A place where he is directing you to go? How will you respond?

4. What key lesson did you glean from today's study?

To recap:

- Faith without deeds is dead.
- Be willing to act when God directs you into someone's life.

Day Four

Don't Run Ahead

Yesterday, we looked at the importance of taking action. Since I'm a take-charge kinda gal, I think taking action is almost always the right choice. I say, when in doubt, gallop. Do something. Anything. When I read the Bible, I find several kindred spirits, including Rebekah.

I like Becky and I'm looking forward to hanging out with her around the glassy sea, someday. She bursts on the scene in Genesis 24 and right away she starts to shake things up and make things happen. When Abraham's servant travels across the desert to find a wife for Isaac, the first person he meets is Rebekah. When he asks her for a drink, she "quickly . . . gave him a drink" (v. 18). The she volunteers to draw enough water for his camels (v. 19). Lest you think that was a small job, it probably required fetching a hundred gallons or more. The jars women carried back then were large enough to carry a full day's supply of water. Yet, she *"ran* back to the well to draw more water" (v. 20, emphasis added). We've got to admire a woman with spunk and a willing spirit.

Rebekah promptly invites the servant and his entourage to spend the night (v. 25) and when he makes the marriage proposal on behalf of Isaac, she instantly accepts (v. 58). Well, I told you she was a woman of action. And, so far, it has worked in her favor. Everything she's done up to this time seems to be in perfect harmony with God's plan. But there comes a time in her life when "running" gets her into trouble, because she runs ahead of God.

When Rebekah is carrying the twins, Jacob and Esau, in her womb, God specifically tells her that Jacob is the chosen heir, even though Esau, as firstborn, was legally entitled to inherit the spiritual and material blessings of his father (Genesis 25:23). So she knows God's plan; she understands the big picture. What she doesn't know is God's timing, and the details of his plan.

When Isaac prepares to pass on the blessing to Esau, Rebekah springs into action. Genesis 27:1–40 recounts Rebekah's elaborate scheme to trick her husband into blessing Jacob. The plot succeeds, all right, and Rebekah once again "shakes things up and makes things happen." Unfortunately, she relies on her own resources and her own cleverness, rather than turning to God. Because she runs ahead of God's plan, Jacob spends much of his life *on the run.* She never sees her son again and the entire family is permanently torn apart.

Rebekah responded to the situation in a crisis-mode. "His mother said to him, 'My son, let the curse fall on me. Just do what I say; go and get them for me'" (Genesis 27:13). She acted out of a sense of panic, as if God's will would be thwarted if she didn't intervene. *God's will is not a crisis!* His eternal plan will come to pass, whether or not we spring into action. God doesn't need us to shake things up and make things happen; he is quite capable of doing that on his own.

We don't know how God might have arranged for Jacob to inherit the blessing. We *do know* that God's purposes must stand and that, in his own timing, he would have granted the blessing to Jacob. And we can be sure he wouldn't have resorted to lies and deception to do so. We also know this: "The blessing of the LORD brings wealth, and he adds no trouble to it" (Proverbs 10:22). Rebekah brought incredible heartache to herself and to her family by running ahead of God and trying to take matters into her own hands.

How about you? Perhaps God has made a specific promise to you, either during prayer or through his Word. But rather than wait for him to fulfill that promise in his way and in his time, you ran ahead and made a mess of things. This pattern has been repeated over and over again in my life. As I shared with you earlier in the book, just days after I accepted Christ, God laid on my heart a vision for my life's work. Time after time, I run ahead and try to "make it happen." Even though the ends I'm trying to accomplish *are in accordance with God's stated will*, he withholds his blessings. Why? Because I'm running ahead.

Are you running ahead of God? Or are you trusting *completely* in the one who promised to work out the details?

1. What do you learn about Rebekah from the way she reacted to Abraham's servant? (If you have time, read Genesis 24; if Rebekah intrigues you—as she does me—read through Genesis 27.)

2. Did her "take charge" personality work in accordance with God's plan? Why or why not?

3. What did God reveal to Rebekah concerning her sons?

4. Was Rebekah right or wrong to be upset when she saw her husband preparing to bless Esau? What might have been going through her mind?

5. Rebekah had the right "ends" in mind. But did the ends justify the means? Why or why not?

6. Rebekah's concerns *were* justified, but how could she have expressed those concerns differently? What might she have done instead of dreaming up the elaborate plot?

7. Have you ever run ahead of God? What was the result?

8. Is there something God has promised you will take place, but you are getting impatient? Are you running ahead of him now? Or are you tempted to run ahead? Describe the promise and why you feel God might need your help to speed things along a bit!

9. How should you handle the situation differently (i.e. rather than taking matters into your own hands)?

10. What key lesson did you glean from today's study?

To recap:

- When we take matters into our own hands, rather than going where God directs, we bring pain to ourselves and to others.
- God's will is not a crisis. It will come to pass whether we spring into action or not.
- Don't run ahead of God. Wait patiently for him to work out the details of what he has promised.

Day Five

Expect the Unexpected

Now that you have come to the end of week nine, you understand the Five Requirements of becoming a vessel God can use. If you are like me, you are eager to discover what God will do next in your life—in order to experience the incredible joy of being used by him. But I have to warn you: you had better expect the unexpected! When you open your life to God, he will use you in the most unexpected ways. Indeed, when you say to him, "Lord, I am ready to pour out my life in sacrificial service, however and wherever you direct," get ready for surprises.

As we close our study for the week, I want to tell you how God has worked in my own life. Earlier, I shared with you about my miscarriage. At that time, I looked around at other couples who had been married as long as we had (twelve years, thirteen now) and had "so much more to show for it." As the Lord brought me through the grieving process and the healing began, I knew there was only one more hurdle left to cross: my original due date, August 29. I filed the date in the back of my mind, but as it drew closer I had to block it out of my conscious thought.

On August 28, a request came through the church prayer chain. A young girl was in need of a home because both of her parents were in jail. She had attended our church youth camp with a friend several weeks earlier and had made a profession of faith in Christ. Unless someone in the church took action, she would become a ward of the state. The moment the caller explained the request, I knew God wanted us to give the girl a home. I called the pastor immediately to tell him as much. He was stunned; we had just sought counseling at the church because our financial problems were so severe they were affecting our marriage. But I stood firm in my conviction and he arranged for me to meet her the next day.

When my husband came home that night, I told him what had transpired. He thought I was absolutely out of my mind. His parents were staying with us at the time, and they, too, thought the entire idea was outrageous. Nevertheless, on August 29, I went to the church to meet Nikki, who presented herself as a sullen and angry young girl. We soon discovered that Nikki had a criminal record and had been involved with drugs, alcohol, and was borderline sexually active. The kicker came when she told me she hated children and dreaded the thought of living with our five-year-old daughter.

So, I did what any sane person would do: I invited her to come live with us. . . .

Over the past three months, as we have poured ourselves into her life, God has transformed her into a lovely, bright young lady before our very eyes. She loves to cook and, in fact, offered to prepare dinner last night and the night before. (If you ever get a chance to taste her tacos, don't pass up the opportunity!) She is taking singing lessons from a wonderful Christian girl at church and has joined the youth choir. She shared the gospel with her brother and persuaded him to attend youth camp, where he, too, accepted Christ. Last night, she brought home a school progress report filled with A's and A+'s . . . and an F for failing to turn in assignments. Oh, well, she's not perfect.

Our "second child" certainly did not come the way we expected, but we are grateful. Most amazing of all, within weeks of Nikki's arrival, I discovered that I was pregnant again. God's timing is truly miraculous. Because he took my baby to heaven early, we had room in our lives for Nikki. (We would not have even considered taking her in if my pregnancy had continued.) We hope to soon have our third child. As we prepare as a family for this exciting event, we are expecting the unexpected—trusting God to give us more than we could ask or imagine.

Throughout this week, we have focused on the importance of pouring out your life where God directs and only where he directs. We saw that it's not enough to find a need and fill it, but rather that we have to listen for God's voice and go with God. We explored the importance of big-picture direction and how understanding who you are is critical to understanding how God wants to use you. Even though God can use anyone, it is easier for him to direct a "meaningful specific" than it is a "wandering generality" who repeatedly misses the mark. We also emphasized being willing to act whenever and wherever God directs; being ready to pour out your life in sacrificial service at a moment's notice. However, there is a danger—and that is running ahead. We can get so excited over the big-picture direction and be so eager to act that we run ahead of God and make a mess of things! Today I shared my personal experience of becoming a mother in the most unexpected way—and we saw that a woman who wants to be a vessel God can use must learn to expect the unexpected from God.

The Fifth Requirement for becoming a vessel God can use is:

Pour out your life in ministry as God directs.

1. What are some unexpected ways that God has used you?

2. What are some things you are "expecting" in your life right now?

3. How will you respond if God responds in an "unexpected" way?

4. What was "This Week's Focus"?

5. What are the five requirements for becoming a vessel God can use?

To recap:

- Expect the unexpected from God.
- Pour your life wherever God directs . . . even if it's not what you had in mind.

Week Ten: Experiencing

This Week's Focus:

Experiencing the Joy of Being a Vessel God Can Use

This Week's Focus Verse:

I am the vine; you are the branches. If a man remains in me
and I in him, he will bear much fruit;
apart from me you can do nothing.

John 15:5

Day One

Where Does Joy Come From?

D o you know the joy of being used by God? Do you know the joy of living exactly the way he created you to live? Do you know the joy of walking by faith, walking in obedience day by day? If you don't know that kind of joy, then you really don't know joy at all. For today, let's meditate on how we can experience the joy that can only flow from the throne of God.

What are some of the ways we can access that joy?

Through obedience: "If you obey my commands, you will remain in my love, just as I have obeyed my Father's commands and remain in his love. I have told you this so that my joy may be in you and *that your joy may be complete* [emphasis added]. My command is this: Love each other as I have loved you. Greater love has no one than this, that one lay down his life for his friends" (John 15:10–13). When we follow Christ, even through the valley, even to the point of laying down our lives, we can experience complete joy.

Through sitting in his presence: "You have made known to me the path of life; you will fill me with joy in your presence, with eternal pleasures at your right hand" (Psalm 16:11). And again, "Surely you have granted him eternal blessings and made him glad with the joy of your presence" (Psalm 21:6). Have you discovered this joy yet? It's so hard for me because I just hate to sit still. Yet, when I went through the sadness of losing my child through miscarriage, I was enveloped by God's presence and experienced the joy that flies in the face of logic. We don't have to wait until a crisis strikes to *stop* long enough to sit and enjoy God's presence. If we'll take the time, he promises to fill us with joy.

Through meditating on God's Word: "The precepts of the LORD are right, giving joy to the heart" (Psalm 19:8). Also, "Your statutes are my heritage forever; they are the joy of my heart. My heart is set on keeping your decrees to the very end" (Psalm 119:111–112). Do you find *joy* in God's Word or do you read it out of duty? Maybe you don't read it at all? If we truly meditate on God's Word, letting it settle down into our hearts and transform us from the inside out, we'll discover what it means for the precepts of the Lord to give joy to the heart.

Through receiving his comfort: "When anxiety was great within me, your consolation brought joy to my soul" (Psalm 94:19). Now, I want you to brace yourself. A wild story is coming and I want you to know *this stuff don't happen 'round these parts—at least, not too often!* Here goes: I went through a very severe depression while writing the book *No More Lone Ranger Moms.* Looking back, I realize I came dangerously close to a nervous breakdown. My theme song was: "Nobody likes me, everybody hates me, think I'll go eat worms."

One Sunday, I was sitting in church cursing myself and the day I was born. My strength was gone from crying for days on end. I had cried until I couldn't cry any more. I had cried until I could barely breathe. I had cried until my face hurt. Have you ever cried like that?

I looked around the church and mumbled to myself, "No one here cares about me. No one here likes me. I hate who I am. Oh, God, how I hate who I am." Just then, I felt someone wrap his arms around me. It was the most all-encompassing, comforting hug I had ever felt. I felt love and warmth flood over me from my head, down over the length of my body.

Then I heard it. For only the third time in my life, I heard God speak in a way that was virtually audible. "I like you, Donna," he whispered. "I like you just the way you are. I love you."

It was *God who hugged me. He reached down to comfort me, he wrapped his heavenly arms around me* and I was flooded with an inexpressible joy. Tears began streaming down my face as I rested in his lingering embrace. My poor husband had no idea what was going on. He only knew I was smiling broadly and producing actual tears. (I think that's the part that really got him. He knew that was a miracle because I couldn't possibly have any tears left.) I was so overwhelmed I had to leave the service in tears. I stood outside the sanctuary for twenty minutes, savoring the joy I felt when my God comforted me.

Now, I can't guarantee you a heavenly hug, but God does guarantee his consolation will bring joy to your soul. When friends cannot be found, the God of all comfort is there. Seek him and you will find him.

Through recalling what God has done: "The LORD has done great things for us, and we are filled with joy" (Psalm 126:3). The next time your joy is on the wane, recall the wonderful things God has already done for you. That's why keeping a "Thankful List" (which we discussed in Week 5) is so important. It's also why knowing God's Word is vital; we can quickly bring to mind God's marvelous deeds on behalf of his people. When we are in need of rescue, we can call to mind Shadrach, Meshach, and Abednego, who were thrown into the fiery furnace but stood firm:

> Shadrach, Meshach and Abednego replied to the king, "O Nebuchadnezzar, we do not need to defend ourselves before you in this matter. If we are thrown into the blazing furnace, the God we serve is able to save us from it, and he will rescue us from your hand, O king. But even if he does not, we want you to know, O king, that we will not serve your gods or worship the image of gold you have set up."   Daniel 3:16–18

I'll bet you know how that story ends. If not, go quick, look it up. It will fill your heart with joy.

Through perseverance during hard times: Hard times come into every life. Barbara Johnson's book title puts it so well: *Pain Is Inevitable, but Misery Is Optional . . . So Stick a Geranium in Your Hat and Be Happy!* Better still, hide God's Word in your heart and be joyful. Whatever it takes, persevere. To those who don't give up when the going gets tough, God promises: "Those who sow in tears will reap with songs of joy. He who goes out weeping, carrying seed to sow, will return with songs of joy, carrying sheaves with him" (Psalm 126:5–6).

Well, we've only looked at a handful of the hundreds of verses concerning joy. Throughout this week, we'll explore the joy that is ours as vessels God can use. Go hug a friend today. And tell them God sent you!

1. What are some ways we can experience joy, according to the Bible. (First draw on your memory, then go back and review the lesson.)

2. Recall a time when you experienced joy despite your circumstances. Describe. Note how it was different from joy you've experienced because of circumstances.

3. One of the deepest joys we can experience is the joy of serving others. The following poem offers some practical ways we can experience joy by bringing joy into the lives of others. Meditate on it and then respond to the questions provided.

"Plant a Garden of Joy"

Plant 5 rows of Peas:
   Prayer, perseverance, politeness, promptness, and purity
Plant 3 rows of Squash:
   Squash gossip, squash criticism, and squash indifference.
Plant 5 rows of Lettuce:
   Let us be faithful to duty; let us be unselfish; let us be truthful; let us follow Christ; let us love one another.
No garden is complete without Turnips:
   Turn up for church; turn up with a smile; turn up with new ideas; turn up with determination to make everything count for something good and worthwhile.

—source unknown

4. Which of the Peas do you need more of? (For each of these, give specific answers and justify each with an example or two.)

5. What do you need to Squash?

6. Does the Lettuce describe you? If not, what changes do you need to make?

7. Do you turn up in a way that brings joy *to others*?

8. What key lesson did you glean from today's study?

To recap:

- We can experience joy in spite of circumstances.
- Some of the deepest joys in life come through serving others.

Day Two

The Joy of Ministry and the Danger of Dashed Expectations

We are not called to a life of glory and honor and leisure. We are called to a life of service, a life of ministry. The moment we forget that, God cannot use us and our joy disappears. We find a perfect illustration of this truth in Mark 10:

> Then James and John, the sons of Zebedee, came to him. "Teacher," they said, "we want you to do for us whatever we ask."
> "What do you want me to do for you?" he asked.
> They replied, "Let one of us sit at your right and the other at your left in your glory."
> "You don't know what you are asking," Jesus said. "Can you drink the cup I drink or be baptized with the baptism I am baptized with?"
> "We can," they answered.
> Jesus said to them, "You will drink the cup I drink and be baptized with the baptism I am baptized with, but to sit at my right or left is not for me to grant. These places belong to those for whom they have been prepared."
> When the ten heard about this, they became indignant with James and John. Jesus called them together and said, "You know that those who are regarded as rulers of the Gentiles lord it over them, and their high officials exercise authority over them. Not so with you. Instead, whoever wants to become great among you must be your servant, and whoever wants to be first must be slave of all. For even the Son of Man did not come to be served, but to serve, and to give his life as a ransom for many."
> Mark 10:37–45

James and John wanted to know who was going to get the best *seats* in the Kingdom. They expected to *sit down* and be served. They expected Jesus to give them the place of honor. The other disciples were indignant. Why? For righteousness sake? Are you kidding? They were indignant because *they expected the place of honor.* How does Jesus respond? "The son of man came not to be served, but to serve." I prefer the King James Version, which reads: "The son of man came not to be ministered unto, but to minister."

If you desire to be a vessel God can use, you've got to come to grips with this truth. There is nothing else on earth that can hinder our effectiveness—and prevent us from experiencing joy in our everyday lives—like an attitude that says, "I have not come to minister, but to be ministered unto. I have not come to serve, but to be served." If we feel this way, we have not known or seen Jesus. We have not understood his message.

Am I overstating the case? Let's explore a few examples and see. Imagine this scenario: Your husband (or significant other) forgets your birthday. You're angry. Why? Because you expected him to minister to you by giving you a gift. Now, that hardly seems like an unrealistic expectation. It certainly wasn't very nice of your husband to forget. But if your whole purpose was to minister to your husband rather than be ministered to, it wouldn't ruffle your feathers so much to be forgotten.

Maybe you are unhappy with your marriage in general. Could it be you have unrealistic expectations about marriage? My husband and I went through a terrible time in our marriage when he was unemployed. Let me tell you, unemployed husbands are pure joy . . . *not*! And I kept thinking, "If only I could ditch this bum, I'd be living with Robert Redford within a week and all my problems would be solved." (Well, I told you we manic-depressives are given to flights of fancy. There were days when I actually believed Bob and I had a chance. Spoooky!)

Well, one night my husband and I had a huge blow-up. We decided to go somewhere to sit undistracted and hash things out. So we went to McDonald's. Can you tell we had a four-year-old? Well, thank God for Playland! Anyway, there we sat, each pointing out how the other had failed. Hadn't lived up to our expectations of what a husband should be or what a wife should be. Finally, my husband said, "Can you name anyone who has a perfect marriage. Can you name anyone who has even a very *good* marriage?"

He had me. It was a simple statement, but it brought me back to reality. Life isn't perfect. So stop expecting it to be. Your husband isn't Robert Redford. And if you married Robert Redford, you'd probably find out that he's not Robert Redford, either. It's not your job to evaluate, educate, or otherwise improve your mate. It's your job to *serve him, to minister to him* and to encourage him to Christlikeness. If you are operating on any other motive, you can expect that old bitter root to sprout any day now. *Adios,* joy!

How about our children? Do we really minister to them? Or do we expect them to minister to us by being model children. We expect them to love the Lord. Get straight A's. Excel in sports. Marry the right person, but not until *we* are ready! Those are all good things, but we have no right to demand them. One of my mother's favorite sayings was, "You ungrateful kids." She had eight of us, so she ought to know. Yes, kids are ungrateful. It comes with the Happy Meals and the Barbie dolls. Sort of a package deal.

I remember one time when my daughter, Leah, was three. God really hammered home this message about ministering to our children. This was also during the time my husband was unemployed. I was working fifteen hours a day—with *no baby-sitter* and no help of any kind. Cameron job-hunted all day, every day, so he was never around to help. I was truly the Lone Ranger Mom! Do you feel sorry for me yet? Gee, why didn't someone *come minister to me?* Oops, didn't mean to say that!

On with the story. My daughter came to me and said, "Mommy, you aren't paying enough attention to me." Out of the mouths of babes! And I thought, "You know, she's right." So I decided we would have a special mother-daughter day. How do you think it worked out?

I let her choose where to go for lunch. First she said, "Burgu King." When we got there, she didn't want "Burgu King," she wanted Pizza Pizza (That's Peter Piper Pizza, for those of you who know the spot. It not only has pizza, but serves as a mini-indoor amusement park, with rides and games, etc.) Well, there's about a gad-zillion of these joints in Arizona, so I decided to just drive around, expecting a Peter Piper Pizza to turn up at any minute. How well do you think that went??

My daughter had been whining in the backseat since we left the house. The drivers behind me were going ballistic because I kept slowing down to check every shopping center for evidence of a Peter

Piper Pizza. This mother-daughter bonding thing was not turning out the way I expected!

Well, finally I found a little mom-and-pop pizza shop and I was feeling desperate. Needless to say, the pizza shop didn't have rides or games or any other fun kid stuff. Talk about dashed expectations. My daughter was not pleased. But she quickly discovered a smoke-filled back room where a bunch of teenagers were playing "kill anything that moves" on the video screen.

She started running around wreaking havoc like she'd just been released from reform school. There I was, gagging on cigarette smoke. The food was taking forever. *I was not in a good mood, people.* I was grumbling about the lousy service and issuing commands while my daughter completely ignored me. So I started chasing her around the restaurant, cursing the day she was born. I was talking to myself *out loud.* About that time a woman came up to me looking rather puzzled and said, "Aren't you . . . Donna Partow? (Pregnant pause.) I attended your seminar last weekend." And I started thinking, "This *fame* thing isn't as great as I expected it to be." My only hope was that she hadn't attended my session on the joy of parenting.

Here's the point: *I wasn't there to minister to my daughter.* Not at all. I expected *her* to minister to *me.* I expected her to cooperate. To reassure me that I could neglect her and not pay any price. I expected her to make me look good in public. Like James and John, I expected the *seat of honor.* When I didn't get it, my joy melted like a pile of mozzarella in a pizza oven.

1. What did James and John want Jesus to do for them? What was the real motive behind their request?

2. Jesus said they had it all wrong. According to Jesus, what should *their desire have been?*

Day Three

The Joy of Ministry . . . Part Two

Today we continue looking at the joy of ministry . . . and the danger of dashed expectations.

Let's look at a few typical examples of this desire to be ministered unto, rather than to minister. How about church? You go, but the service is dull. The sermon puts you to sleep. You expected to be energized for the coming week. You expected to get your spiritual fix. And you're disappointed. No one greeted you after the service. No one even mentioned your mother's surgery, which you asked them to pray about. You are hurt and you harbor your right to be hurt like a treasured possession. Why? Because you went to be ministered to, rather than to minister. *Sianara*, joy!

Even in our ministry efforts, this attitude creeps in and wreaks havoc. Why do people burn out? Why do we drop out? We expect to see results and when they're not forthcoming, we give up. We expect people to thank us, to admire us, *to give us the seat of honor*. And when they don't, we're angry and bitter. Just remember, the son of man did not come to be served, but to serve and to give his life as a ransom for many. We must do the same.

Isn't it amazing how we can enter a ministry with the best of intentions and end up getting sidetracked? Isn't it amazing *how our motives can muddy the waters*? I know I have to constantly examine my motives, to figure out why I am doing what I'm doing. Just a few moments ago, the special events chairperson from our church called and asked me to speak at the Christmas dinner. Well, the last time they asked me to speak, I replied, "I would rather be stripped naked, paraded through the streets, tarred and feathered, then dipped in kerosene and set on fire." Why? Because Jesus said, "No prophet is accepted in his hometown" (Luke 4:24), and I know he's right!

I had every intention of saying "No way" again this year, because when I speak, *I want to be accepted.* I want to be loved and honored. I want the audience to minister to me. I want them to tell me how great I am and, most of all, I want them to buy my books. *Can you believe I just admitted that?*

Sitting in church last Sunday, I opened the church bulletin and saw a list of upcoming women's ministry events. There it was: the December 7 Christmas gig with an unidentified speaker and I thought, "Oh no, they're gonna ask me again." And the Holy Spirit responded, "This time you will say yes." I pointed out the Luke 4 passage, but apparently God wasn't impressed. "Now you're catching on, Donna. You're not *supposed to get the honor. You're supposed to obey me.*"

In my heart I knew, *God is calling me to minister to the women of my church*, even if they don't minister to me in return. Even if they don't love me, even if they don't tell me what a great job I did, and yes, even if they don't buy my books. God is calling me to minister, not to be ministered unto.

God is hammering this home so hard, I just know there are women reading this book who need to hear these words. Throughout the past several weeks, a number of people in a wide range of situations have come up to me and said, "I heard you speak" or, "I read your book." Gee, that's nice, but what's it worth? Do I write to earn the dollar per book I get paid? How pathetic! Or is there something far more important than earning a royalty check, something more important than *having been read.*

I am coming to realize that if you walk away from this study saying, "I read Donna Partow's book," *I will have completely failed you.* I will have completely failed to be a vessel God can use. Did you really pick up this book to read what Donna Partow typed up in her home office? Didn't you pick it up so that you could become a vessel God can use? Didn't you undertake this study to learn more *of God, to be drawn closer to him?*

Reading Donna Partow's book means nothing. It means less than nothing, unless it becomes a vessel through which God himself can communicate. You set this book before you during your daily Quiet Time, expecting the God of the Universe to communicate with you through it. Your goal is to listen for God's voice, and if he can't speak through me, if all I do is get in the way and draw attention to myself and my ideas and my opinions, what's the point?

I beg of you to examine your own life and ministry. Are you operating as a vessel God can use *to draw people to himself* or are you *just drawing attention to yourself?* Once more with feeling, ladies! Do your ministry efforts draw people to God—or do they merely draw people to you? I hate to break the news, but if you are simply drawing attention to yourself (i.e. wanting to be ministered unto, rather than to minister), major trouble looms ahead for you. Because God will not share his glory with another. He will not share his glory with me, and he will not share it with you. If that means shutting down your ministry, he'll do it in a heartbeat. Believe me, I *know.*

Let me give you a little self-test you can take before starting any ministry project or doing any good deed. *Ask yourself: Can I do this without expecting anything in return?* If the answer is no, don't do it. Whether you expect a thank-you note, praise, approval, a plaque, or a wing of the church named after you, if you expect anything at all—other than to hear from your Master's lips, "Well done, good and faithful servant"—*don't do it.* If you enter into ministry with a secret desire to *be ministered unto rather than to minister*, your efforts will bring you heartache rather than joy. What's worse, they may bring dishonor to your Lord in the process.

Try this out the next time you're feeling angry, bitter, resentful, jealous, frustrated, disappointed—anything but joyful: Ask yourself the following five questions and see if your joy returns:

1. What is preventing me from experiencing the maximum joy possible in this situation? Understanding the reason for your joylessness is the first step to recovering it.

2. What expectations do I have about the person or circumstance that is stealing my joy? Are those expectations realistic?

3. Is my core desire to minister—or to be ministered unto? And remember, there's nothing wrong with being ministered to. Jesus was refreshed and ministered to; so was Paul. But don't expect it. God knows your need. He is your Jehovah-Jireh and he will provide.

4. Am I willing to be used by God in and through this situation? No matter how inconvenient or difficult?

5. Am I willing to let God use whatever tools—whatever husband, whatever children, whatever church—whatever circumstances he chooses to transform me into a vessel he can use. Whether it's

something as seemingly insignificant as a long line at the grocery store checkout or something as devastating as the death of a child.

Ask yourself those five questions every time you feel your joy slipping away. See what a difference a change in perspective can make.

1. Think of a situation (church assignment, relationship, etc.) where you started out with "good intentions" but ended up feeling bitter? (Indeed, many situations may come to mind.) Looking back, what was your real goal?

2. Bring that situation before the Lord. Confess and receive his forgiveness.

3. Give examples of conflict or discontent in your daily life that you now recognize is rooted in the desire to be ministered to. Note how you can adopt a more Christlike, servant attitude.

4. What five questions are you going to ask yourself the next time you feel your joy slipping away?

5. Who should you be ministering to? Name names. Indicate how your expectations of "being ministered to" have hurt these relationships in the past and what changes you can make.

6. What key lesson did you glean from today's study?

To recap:

- Our calling is to minister to others, not to be ministered unto. When we lose sight of that truth, we lose our joy.
- When we expect others to minister to us we forfeit the joy God intends for us to experience.

Day Four

Remain in Christ

I t is only fitting that, in this final week of our journey together, we will focus on one of Christ's final messages to his disciples. Today, we look at the instructions he gave them shortly before his crucifixion:

> I am the true vine and my Father is the gardener. He cuts off every branch in me that bears no fruit, while every branch that does bear fruit he trims clean so that it will be even more fruitful. You are already clean because of the word I have spoken to you. Remain in me, and I will remain in you. No branch can bear fruit by itself; it must remain in the vine. Neither can you bear fruit unless you remain in me.
>
> I am the vine; you are the branches. If a man remains in me and I in him, he will bear much fruit; apart from me you can do nothing. If anyone does not remain in me, he is like a branch that is thrown away and withers; such branches are picked up, thrown into the fire and burned. If you remain in me and my words remain in you, ask whatever you wish, and it will be given you. This is to my Father's glory, that you bear much fruit, showing yourselves to be my disciples.
>
> As the Father has loved me, so have I loved you. Now remain in my love. If you obey my commands, you will remain in my love, just as I have obeyed my Father's commands and remain in his love. I have told you this so that my joy may be in you and that your joy may be complete. My command is this: Love each other as I have loved you. Greater love has no one than this, that one lay down his life for his friends. You are my friends if you do what I command. John 15:1–14

If you have faithfully persevered to this point in the study—examining God's Word and meditating on key scriptures—no doubt you've grown in your faith. Now you've learned what you need to know, so it's just a simple matter of getting out there and gettin' the job done for God. Right? Well, not quite.

I'm almost embarrassed to admit this, but that's what I thought the Christian life was all about, until very recently. I thought you found out what you were supposed to do—through a sermon, a Bible study, or your own Quiet Time—and then you did it. If you did a good job, God would be proud of you. If you blew it (and, of course, I almost always blew it), he'd lower the heavenly hammer.

Actually, that's what most religions boil down to. We perform on earth's stage while God watches passively, rating us on a scale of one to ten. Some of America's most popular religions teach that God now "grades on a curve." That is to say, as long as you're not much worse than everyone else, you should be able to slip into heaven.

However, all such performance-based religions are man-made. Genuine Christianity is not about performance, it's about a relationship. It's about the God of the universe reaching down and initiating a personal love relationship with sinful people like you and me. Although we usually acknowledge that we came to know Christ through the wooing of the Holy Spirit, our daily lives often fail to reflect an ongoing love relationship with God.

Notice again a theme we've hit upon throughout this study: When we bear fruit as a natural extension of our life in Christ, *it is to the Father's glory*. And why does God want us to bring him glory? Again, is it a heavenly ego trip? No! He wants men to *see that we are his disciples, so that they, too, will desire to become his disciples*. We may not think it's the most efficient method, *but this is the method God has chosen to reach the world*.

The whole reason God created you and me is that we might reflect his glory and enjoy a love relationship with him. When we go about "doing great things for God" in our own strength, we rob God of his glory. Far from being pleased with us, Jesus says the Father will *cut us off*. The last thing God needs is another glory-seeker in the church; Satan has already planted enough of those in all the strategic places.

If we want to bear fruit—which is another way of saying, if we want to be a vessel God can use—we must remain in close fellowship with Christ. He is the vine. He is the source of life. The moment we walk away and start working as an *independent contractor*, we have cut ourselves off from the very source of our life. Not only will we not produce fruit, it's just a matter of time before we wither and die.

You may get the impression from today's passage that God is a great big meanie, roaming the church with a hatchet, just waiting for someone to slip up. Nothing could be further from the truth. He only cuts off those branches that are already dead. He does so for one reason only: for the sake of the entire tree (i.e. the Church). A dead branch can never produce fruit again, but it can prevent other branches from producing fruit. Haven't you noticed that someone who is spiritually dead is one of the greatest hindrances to God's work?

Jesus promises that as long as we remain in him, we will produce fruit and remain in the Father's love. That's not to say we won't have to go through the pruning process, a process that lasts throughout our entire life. But we have the assurance that *the only reason* God allows these pruning experiences is so that we will be even more fruitful.

Why is Jesus telling us all this stuff about vines and fruit and pruning? "I have told you this so that my joy may be in you and that your joy may be complete." Don't you know this to be true? There is no greater joy in life than knowing you are fulfilling the very reason for your existence. When your life brings glory to God and you walk in a close love relationship with him, nothing on earth can steal your joy.

Remain in him and he will remain in you. Then your joy will be complete.

1. What does it mean to "remain in Christ"? Give practical examples from your everyday life of how you can practice remaining in him.

2. Do you live as if you honestly believe that apart from Christ you can do absolutely nothing *of lasting value?*

3. How would your life be different if you lived according to the knowledge that apart from Christ you can do nothing of lasting value? Be specific!

4. What does Jesus say is the secret to experiencing complete joy? Have you ever experienced that kind of joy? When?

5. What key lesson did you glean from today's study?

To recap:

- Christ is the vine—the very source of our life. We must remain in close fellowship with him.
- Apart from Christ, we can do absolutely nothing of value in God's Kingdom.
- Our joy will be complete when we bear much fruit.

Day Five

The Joy Set Before You

Throughout this week, we've talked about experiencing joy in the Christian life. We should not expect a superficial joy, though. Jesus, the perfect vessel for the Father to accomplish his purposes on earth, modeled a rather unpopular lifestyle:

- born in a stable
- lived in poverty
- scorned by the savvy
- loved by the ignorant
- companion of sinners
- betrayed by a friend
- abandoned by the people he trusted most
- hounded and finally executed by those in power

And why did Jesus endure all of this? *For the joy set before him.* What joy was that? Was it the joy of hearing men's applause? No. Was it the joy of having "everything turning up roses"? No. Was it the joy of winning a popularity contest? No. It was the deep and abiding joy that only comes when we allow the Father to accomplish his work through us. It is the joy that can only come when we are truly *a vessel God can use. It is the joy that comes when we look only to eternity for our rewards.*

> Let us fix our eyes on Jesus, the author and perfecter of our faith, who for the joy set before him endured the cross, scorning its shame, and sat down at the right hand of the throne of God. Consider him who endured such opposition from sinful men, so that you will not grow weary and lose heart.   Hebrews 12:2–3

As you journey on to become a vessel God can use, be prepared for hard times, *but keep the joy set before you.* Expect opposition from sinful men—and that includes people within every church and every ministry—*but keep the joy set before you.* It is the joy that will spare you from burn-out and bitterness. It is the joy that will keep you from growing weary or losing heart. It is the joy that is uniquely ours as we conform our lives to his will and yield ourselves to become a vessel God can use.

> May God himself, the God of peace, sanctify you through and through. May your whole spirit, soul and body be kept blameless at the coming of our Lord Jesus Christ. The one who calls you is faithful and he will do it.   1 Thessalonians 5:23–24

I can hardly believe we've come to the end of our ten weeks together. I invite you now to set aside time to reflect on the lessons God has taught you.

1. Do you know who God is? What, specifically, have you learned about his character, his Word, his will, and his ways?

2. Have you gained an increased understanding of who you are and why God fashioned you as he did? More importantly, do you accept the person God created you to be? Have you stopped quarreling with your Maker?

3. Are you willing to be emptied of self—to let go of your hidden agenda, your secret longings, your hopes and dreams—so that you might be filled with God?

4. Are you willing to be cleansed—even if the process is painful? Are you willing to purify yourself through a life of confession and repentance?

5. Are you willing to be filled and constantly refilled, so that you will have something of God to offer others?

6. Have you learned to listen more carefully for God's voice? Are you willing to follow where he leads?

7. Is your heart's desire to be a vessel God can use? Express that in a written prayer to the Father:

8. What key lesson did you glean from today's study?

9. What was "This Week's Focus"?

To recap:

- Jesus endured Calvary *for the joy set before him.*
- Fix your eyes on Jesus. No matter what obstacles you face, as you seek to become a vessel God can use, press on. And always remember *the joy set before you.*

Five Requirements for Becoming
A Vessel God Can Use

ACCEPT
the way God made you.

Be *EMPTIED* of self
to make room for God.

Allow God to *CLEANSE* you
even if the process is painful.

Be *FILLED* and constantly refilled
with the Living Water of the Holy Spirit.

POUR OUT your life
in ministry *as God directs.*

A Note to Leaders

Thank you for taking on the challenge of leading others through this study *Becoming a Vessel God Can Use*. I pray that this experience will lead you into a closer walk with God and deeper fellowship with those who participate. On the following pages, you will find handouts designed to help you and your group members get the most out of this study. *Be sure to make several photocopies of all forms before writing on them!* Here are some suggestions on how to use these resources:

Participant Profile Sheet

Ask the participants to complete a Profile Sheet during your first meeting. Allow plenty of time for this exercise—the insight you will gain will be extremely valuable as you seek to meet the needs of each woman. Once everyone has finished, spend time discussing their responses *but do not call on anyone*. People do not like to be "put on the spot" so let them know from the beginning that your policy is to encourage—but not require—participation in the discussion.

Make it a point to contact each woman on a regular basis *outside the "classroom"* environment. It could be a phone call, a note card, or a trip to the park together. The key is to demonstrate a personal interest in their spiritual growth and well-being. The Profile Sheets will give you a good place to start in understanding each woman's needs and initiating conversation.

Prayer Requests

In my experience, prayer time in women's groups can quickly deteriorate into idle chit-chat or a gripe session—with twenty minutes discussing "requests" and two minutes spent in actual prayer. *Prayer changes things; building up to prayer accomplishes little.* Tell the women at the first meeting that you intend to spend prayer time *in prayer*. To facilitate that, provide each woman with several copies of the Prayer Request form. Encourage them to write out their requests during the week and also allow time at the beginning of each class for women to complete the Prayer Request forms and turn them in to you.

Once you have collected all of the forms, quickly check to see if any items are marked "Teacher Only" and set those aside. Divide the rest of the slips among women who indicate a willingness to pray aloud.

Prayer Log

In addition to the prayer request slips, I've also provided a master Prayer Log. Each week, after your meeting, add the new prayer requests to your ongoing log. Once you've done so, you can toss out the slips. If you need to maintain a handwritten log, be sure to use black ink. If you (or someone in your class) can maintain the Prayer Log on a computer, that would be ideal!

You can keep the Prayer Log up to date when you make personal contact with the women outside of class. Also encourage the women to call you anytime to add, update or eliminate prayer requests. If you have access to a copy machine, you can photocopy the list each week before you gather, so each woman will have a complete list of prayer concerns. If you don't have a copy machine, let each member maintain *her own* Prayer Log and simply take a few minutes at the beginning of prayer time to bring everyone up to date.

Memory Verse Cards (with key thoughts)

Here's the one exception to the "no putting people on the spot" rule. Each week, at the very beginning of class, ask each woman to recite her verse from memory. Do it in a spirit of fun and out of a desire to "spur one another on toward love and good deeds." Do be sensitive and avoid embarrassing anyone. Nevertheless, when the women come to understand that they will be expected to recite their verse, *almost all* will rise to the occasion and put in the extra effort.

If women will carry their memory verse cards with them wherever they go, there is absolutely no reason why they can't memorize one verse per week. You may find it helpful to review the tips provided in Week Three, Day Five: "Know God's Word by Heart." Using these techniques, anyone can learn to memorize scripture effectively.

Along with each week's memory verse, I have also included two or three key thoughts that summarize the lesson. These do not have to be memorized but will help the women get the most out of the study.

Prayer Request   Date: _____

Submitted by:_____

_____

_____

_____

☐ Teacher only   ☐ Full class

Prayer Request   Date: _____

Submitted by: _____

_____

_____

_____

☐ Teacher only   ☐ Full class

Prayer Request   Date: _____

Submitted by: _____

_____

_____

_____

☐ Teacher only   ☐ Full class

Prayer Request   Date: _____

Submitted by: _____

_____

_____

_____

☐ Teacher only   ☐ Full class

Participant Profile

Name _____   Phone _____

Address _____

_____

Reason for enrolling in this class _____

_____

What is the most pressing problem/challenge in your life right now?

_____

_____

How can this class (and your fellow classmates) help you cope more effectively?

_____

_____

How do you want your life to be different at the end of this study?

_____

_____

What are some specific character traits you would like to see strengthened?

_____

_____

_____

What are some specific habits you want to improve?

_____

_____

_____

_____

List five things you expect from a women's Bible study. (Indicate things you like/dislike)

_____

_____

_____

_____

_____

Thinking back on prior experiences with Bible studies, what motivates you to finish a class? What might cause you to drop out?

_____

_____

_____

_____

How can your leader help you to get the most out of this class?

_____

_____

_____

Prayer Log

Date	Name	Request	Update/Praise

Week 1: Isaiah 55:8-9

"For my thoughts are not your thoughts, neither are your ways my ways," declares the LORD. "As the heavens are higher than the earth, so are my ways higher than your ways and my thoughts than your thoughts." (NIV)

Becoming a Vessel God Can Use, Donna Partow

Week 2: 2 Chronicles 16:9

For the eyes of the LORD range throughout the earth to strengthen those whose hearts are fully committed to him. (NIV)

Becoming a Vessel God Can Use, Donna Partow

Week 3: Exodus 15:11,13

Who among the gods is like you, O LORD? Who is like you--majestic in holiness, awesome in glory, working wonders? In your unfailing love you will lead the people you have redeemed. (NIV)

Becoming a Vessel God Can Use, Donna Partow

Week 4: 2 Corinthians 5:17-18

Therefore, if anyone is in Christ, he is a new creation; the old has gone, the new has come! All this is from God, who reconciled us to himself through Christ and gave us the ministry of reconciliation. (NIV)

Becoming a Vessel God Can Use, Donna Partow

Week 5: Philippians 2:3-4

Do nothing out of selfish ambition or vain conceit, but in humility consider others better than yourselves. Each of you should look not only to your own interests, but also to the interests of others. (NIV)

Becoming a Vessel God Can Use, Donna Partow

Week 6: 1 John 1:9

If we claim to be without sin, we deceive ourselves and the truth is not in us. If we confess our sins, he is faithful and just to forgive us our sins and to purify us from all unrighteousness. (NIV)

Becoming a Vessel God Can Use, Donna Partow

Week 3: Getting to Know the Potter

- When we behold the majesty of our God, it inspires us to want to know him more.
- God's character demonstrates that he does not need us, yet he chooses to accomplish his purposes through our lives.

Week 6: Allowing God to Cleanse You

- God uses people and trials to cleanse us.
- Prayer, meditation, confession, and repentance are central to the cleansing process. So is silence.

Week 2: A Vessel Depends on God Alone

- Self-confidence is trust in my own ability to handle people and circumstances.
- God-confidence is trust in God's ability to work through me to shape people and circumstances.
- Our lives should demonstrate that we are relying on God alone to take care of us.

Week 5: Be Emptied...to Make Room for God

- We must be emptied of the pride and pain of the past.
- We must be emptied of our dreams for the future.

Week 1: God Uses Imperfect Vessels

- You do not have to be perfect to become a vessel God can use.
- God often chooses the most unlikely people to accomplish his purposes.

Week 4: God's Chosen Vessel

- Don't compare yourself. God made you into exactly the kind of vessel he wanted you to be.
- God looks at the heart. His judgment is based not on where we are but how far we've come.

Week 7: Ephesians 5:18-20

Be filled with the Spirit. Speak to one another with psalms, hymns and spiritual songs. Sing and make music in your heart to the Lord, always giving thanks to God the Father for everything, in the name of our Lord Jesus Christ. (NIV)

Becoming a Vessel God Can Use, Donna Partow

Week 8: Psalm 130: 5-6

I wait for the LORD, my soul waits, and in his word I put my hope. My soul waits for the Lord more than watchmen wait for the morning, more than watchmen wait for the morning. (NIV)

Becoming a Vessel God Can Use, Donna Partow

Week 9: Psalm 90:12

Teach us to number our days aright, that we may gain a heart of wisdom. (NIV)

Becoming a Vessel God Can Use, Donna Partow

Week 10: John 15:5

I am the vine; you are the branches. If a man remains in me and I in him, he will bear much fruit; apart from me you can do nothing. (NIV)

Becoming a Vessel God Can Use, Donna Partow

Week 7: A Vessel Must Be Filled

- A vessel cannot produce water. It can only pour forth that which has been poured into it.
- We must be filled with the Living Water, not just good doctrine and religious rituals.

Week 8: Waiting to Hear God's Voice

- God still speaks to his people. If you can't hear him, you are in trouble at the heart of your Christian life.
- God speaks through his Word, prayer, people, and circumstances.

Week 9: Pouring Your Life Where God Directs

- God isn't trying to keep secrets. He wants to communicate his will to you.
- Be willing to take action; but don't run ahead of God.
- When we set aside the Sabbath, we take time to reflect and refill.

Week 10: Experiencing the Joy of Being Used by God

- Jesus endured Calvary for the joy set before him.
- When we expect others to minister to us (rather than seeking to minister) we forfeit our joy.
- Fix your eyes on Jesus. No matter what obstacles you face as you seek to become a vessel God can use, press on. And always remember the joy set before you.